The
Single-Stock Futures
Revolution

The Single-Stock Futures Revolution

Winning Strategies That Leverage
Modest Dollars to Millions
Using Wall Street's Newest Weapon!

Bill Johnson

21st Century Investor Publishing, Inc.

Published by 21st Century Investor Publishing, Inc.
1900 Glades Road Suite 441 Boca Raton FL 33431

ISBN 0-9718048-1-8

Library of Congress Control Number: 2002111642

Printed in the United States of America.

This publication is designed to provide accurate and authoritative information in regard to the subject matter covered. It is provided with the understanding that the publisher is not engaged in rendering legal, accounting or other professional services. If legal advice is required, the services of a competent professional person should be sought. — From a Declaration of Principles, jointly adopted by Committee of American Bar Association and Committee of Publishers and Associations

Although both the author and 21st Century Investor Publishing, Inc. believe the information, data, and contents presented are accurate, they neither represent or guarantee the accuracy and completeness nor assume any liability. It should not be assumed that the methods, techniques, or indicators presented in this book will be profitable or that they will not result in losses. Trading involves the risk of loss, as well as the potential for profit. Past performance is not a guarantee of future results.

CONTENTS

Chapter 1
The Basics of Futures Contracts

There are few things in the investing world that carry such a bad reputation, without justification, as futures contracts. If you ask most people what a futures contract is, they will usually say something like, "I'm not sure, but I know they are very risky and complicated" or "They're just a form of legalized gambling." These beliefs seem to dominate most of the information that is ever passed along to interested investors and, consequently, they've become regarded as truths in the investment world. This is the one regrettable reason why most investors do not take the time to understand futures contracts.

If you fall into this category, whether you are one of the people spreading the rumor or just an unlucky one who's heard it, understand that those "truths" are false and that futures contracts will play a vital role in your upcoming investments. If you don't believe that futures contracts will ever be important to you, or if you're afraid of the "risk" they carry, then ask yourself why you have used other forms of them in the past and found them beneficial!

While I may not be 100% sure that you have used futures contracts, I'm pretty sure you have. But I am certain that, if you did use them, you're happy you did. That's because futures contracts, or other forms of them, are used to remove risk, and people like to get rid of uncertainty. If you would like to eliminate the choppiness in the markets, then futures contracts may be the fastest, cheapest, and most efficient way to do it.

In order to understand how and why you should use them, you must be willing to forget everything you've ever heard about futures contracts so you can learn with an unbiased mind. I will start with the basics of futures and lead up to a brand-new investment tool — single-stock futures — that you will find, in many situations, to be the most cash-efficient way to invest or speculate. Those who finish this book will gain knowledge of the strategies of the most important and revolutionary financial tool we will see for years to come.

Single-stock futures (SSFs), as the name implies, are futures contracts traded on individual stocks, rather than on commodities such as pork bellies and soybeans. Because of this new financial innovation, you will be able to invest or speculate in futures contracts on companies you're already familiar with such as Microsoft, Intel, and IBM.

Before we get into the specifics of single-stock futures (SSFs), let's go over some basics of futures contracts to find out what they are and how they work. Then we'll show you how their benefits can be transferred to your stock portfolio.

First of all, futures contracts are actually one of many classes of *derivatives* — assets whose value is derived from another asset, called the *underlying* asset.

As with any derivative instrument, there can be significant risks. Futures can be risky, but their riskiness depends on how they are used. The fact that they can be risky, however, is not a valid excuse to avoid learning about them. Driving your car can be risky, too, but you probably drive nearly every day without hesitation. It all depends on the risks you allow yourself to take that determine if driving your car — or investing in futures — is too risky. In fact, you may have encountered the "investment pyramid" at some point when reading about investing. This is a graphic description of the various asset classes with the risk and returns increasing as you move up the pyramid. A simplified version appears in Figure 1.1:

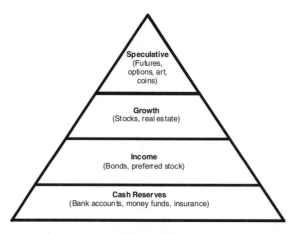

Figure 1.1

The idea is to start your investment portfolio at the bottom of the pyramid and then work your way up to higher yielding assets as your portfolio grows. And there, sitting at the very top, are futures contracts. Once again, this is really a misconception as its position at the top assumes you are using them for speculating, not hedging. In fact, we could turn the pyramid around and make the "safe" bonds in the second tier speculative by shorting them. Shorting an asset simply means the trader sells the asset first with the expectation of buying it back later for a profit due to a decrease in price. Notice how we can take a "safe" bond in the lower portion of the pyramid and send it straight to the top by "going short." The risk depends on how they are used. Keep this in mind as you read through the book, and you will certainly see many conservative uses for these "risky" assets in you own portfolio.

So What Exactly Is a Futures Contract?

Definition: A futures contract is an agreement today to buy or sell something in the future at a predetermined price.

That's all there is to it. As stated earlier, you've probably entered into a futures contract at some time in your life without even knowing it. Let's see how that may have happened.

Think of situations you may have been in that fit the definition. Have you ever purchased a car from a dealer that had to be ordered from the factory? Did you ever sign a contract to purchase a house that wasn't yet built? These examples are, in a sense, nothing more than futures contracts. We agree on the price today but do not pay for it or take delivery until some time in the future. In most cases, we are required to place a small deposit as a show of good faith, but the real money doesn't change hands until the future date. Magazine subscriptions, C.O.D. packages, and layaways are other forms of "futures" contracts.

Let's look at one of these examples a little closer. Assume you want the new convertible Lexus, but your local dealers are sold out. That won't keep a dealer from selling you one, though — he can simply enter into a futures contract with you. Although car dealers won't refer to these agreements as futures contracts, that's basically what they are. The salesman may say, "I don't have that car on the lot right now but I can order one for you. It will take about three months before it arrives." If you agree, the salesman will require a small deposit, maybe as low as a couple hundred bucks, and have you sign an agreement saying that you will pay a certain amount for it when it arrives in three months. That's a futures contract. You both agreed to buy and sell something today for a predetermined price, but payment and delivery will not occur until a later time.

So why would you do such a speculative and reckless thing as enter into a futures contract? Hopefully you see that it's not speculative in this case. You wanted the car today but the dealer didn't have it. If you wait for three months for the next shipment to arrive, you are running the risk of prices moving higher (after all, the fact that he is sold out suggests that there is excess demand and prices may rise). By signing the contract and placing a small deposit, you are locking in your purchase price and have removed all unwanted risk of higher prices associated with waiting for the new cars to arrive. At the same time, you will not benefit if the car price should fall, but that obviously is not a concern of yours, otherwise you wouldn't have signed the contract.

The car dealer, on the other hand, faces the *opposite set of risks*. The dealer is at risk if prices fall (or if you go somewhere else to purchase), so he wants to guarantee the sale today and lock in his profits. It is important to understand that the futures contract is made possible because each of you is facing opposite risks. You face the risk of rising prices and the dealer faces the risk of falling prices. Entering into a futures contract with the dealer accomplishes two important things:

- For the dealer, the futures contract locks in profits
- For you, the futures contract controls costs

Futures contracts were designed to remove unwanted risks associated with unforeseen future events. They exist for the very reason why you and your car dealer are willing to lock in a price today for delivery in the future. If that sounds like a good thing, then maybe the futures contract is not such a bad idea. In fact, as you learn more, you will probably agree that the futures contract is probably the most important and successful financial innovation ever.

Maybe there is a way for you to use them in your financial portfolios after all?

Futures and Forwards

On a technical note, futures contracts are exchange traded and are standardized as to the size and quality of the underlying asset. The car example we just gave is really what's called a *forward* agreement since it is not a standardized contract traded on an exchange — that contract for the car was privately negotiated by two independent people. You and the car dealer were completely free to set the delivery date, deposit amounts, and other contract specifications, which is a really nice benefit of forward agreements. Their drawback is that they are often illiquid, meaning that if you must get out of your contract, you may have to take a substantially reduced price to get someone to buy it from you, assuming the contract is even transferable. With forward agreements, you're also at risk of default by the other party and you must make sure you're dealing with someone reputable who can "make good" on the contract — especially if the contract moves against him.

Futures contracts, on the other hand, are cleared through well-capitalized clearing firms so there is no risk of default by the other party. The clearing firm becomes the buyer to every seller and the seller to every buyer. Futures contracts are standardized as to size, quality, delivery dates and all other contract specifications with one exception — price — which is left for the market to decide. Whether standardization is good or bad is a matter of debate, and there are certainly pros and cons to each side. Standardization is good in that it provides a lot of liquidity but not so good in that it creates inflexible terms. To understand what we mean by inflexible terms, take a look at the "random length lumber" contract at the Chicago Mercantile Exchange (CME). This futures contract is an agreement to buy and sell random lengths of 2x4s between 8 and 20 feet. According to the rules of the CME, the following box shows how rigorous they are in defining exactly what is a deliverable grade of lumber. The deliverable grades through May 2002 are described as follows:

**Deliverable Random Length Lumber For
Contract Months Through May 2002**

Each delivery unit shall consist of nominal 2x4s of random lengths from 8 feet to 20 feet. Each delivery unit shall consist of and be grade stamped CONSTRUCTION AND STANDARD, STANDARD AND BETTER, or #1 or #2; however, in no case may the quantity of Standard grade or #2 grade exceed 50%. Each delivery unit shall be manufactured in California, Idaho, Montana, Nevada, Oregon, Washington, Wyoming, or Alberta or British Columbia, Canada, and contain lumber produced from and grade stamped Hem-Fir (except that Hem-Fir shall not be deliverable if it is manufactured in Canada; nor that portion of Washington including and to the west of Whatcom, Skagit, Snohomish, King, Pierce, Lewis and Skamania counties; nor that portion of Oregon including and to the west of Multnomah, Clackamas, Marion, Linn, Lane, Douglas and Jackson counties; nor that portion of California west of Interstate Highway 5 nor south of US Highway 50), Englemann Spruce, Lodgepole Pine, Englemann Spruce/Lodgepole Pine and/or Spruce Pine Fir (except that Spruce-Pine-Fir shall not be deliverable if it is manufactured in those portions of Washington, Oregon and California that are noted above).

Inflexible to say the least, but on the other hand, the quality of the lumber will be consistent regardless of who is making the delivery. You may hear the terms *forwards* and *futures* from time to time — just be aware that they are basically the same thing. Futures contracts are just standardized forward contracts.

Futures Are Not Options

Traders new to futures often confuse them with options. While there are such things as *options on futures* (which we'll talk about in Chapter 8), futures contracts themselves are not options. There are several key differences.

First, with a long futures contract, you *must* buy the underlying asset at expiration unless you enter an offsetting position. With a call option, you have the right but not the obligation to buy the underlying asset. That's a subtle but potentially big difference.

If a futures trader does not wish to take delivery of the underlying asset, he must enter an offsetting contract. An offsetting position is simply the purchase or sale of the same contract, which reverses the obligation. If you initially purchased a March futures contract, the sale of the same March futures contract is a reversing or offsetting position. Because futures use standardized contracts and a clearing firm to match up buyers and sellers, they provide a really big advantage over forward contracts by allowing a quick "escape" if you should desire to get out.

Compare this to a long call option owner. If a long call option owner wishes to not take delivery, they simply do not exercise the contract. There is no need to enter an offsetting position. Even if a long call is in-the-money by more than 3/4 of a point, a simple phone call to your broker can prevent the automatic exercise that otherwise would occur. Remember, with futures contracts you are entering into agreements to either buy or sell the asset in the future. You are not entering into an agreement to give someone the option to do so.

Because the buyer of the option has the right and not the obligation to purchase the underlying asset, he must pay for this right by paying additional money over and above the cost of carry. For example, a one-year $100 call option will be worth at least $5 if interest rates are 5%, since that is the foregone interest that could be earned on the $100. However, we would likely see this call trading for much higher than $5, perhaps $12. While it is true that the option will lose the entire $12 in value if the stock is $100 or lower at expiration, it is the additional $7, in this example, paid by the option buyer that separates it from the futures contract. Again, futures contracts do not contain a time premium above their cost of carry, while options usually do. We'll discuss this further in Chapter 4 when we examine the pricing of futures contracts.

So while options provide limited downside risk, they come at a price. That price is called "time decay," which simply means the option may lose significant value over time even if the underlying asset does not move (or moves in the wrong direction). This is not true for futures contracts.

A second difference between futures and options is that futures contracts will always have a value to them (please don't confuse that with profit). Options, on the other hand, will be worth $0 if they are out-of-the-money at expiration. Futures must have a value, since you are entering a contract to buy and sell the underlying asset in the future. As you will see later, the futures contract must converge to the spot price (the price for immediate delivery) of the underlying asset at expiration. Only if the spot market becomes worthless will a futures contract be worthless at expiration. Futures contracts behave like very deep-in-the-money options.

Third, futures do not have strike prices like options do. If the underlying asset is trading for $100, you may see three-month options with strike prices of $80 through $110 in $5 increments. Whichever strike you buy, that just means you have the right, but not the obligation, to buy or sell the underlying asset for that strike price. Futures contracts, on the other hand, do not have strike prices. You cannot, for example, buy a March $100 futures contract. You could only buy the March contract. The price at which you agree to purchase the underlying asset is effectively your strike price.

When and Why Did Futures Trading Begin?

The earliest futures contract was recorded in 1851, although evidence of forward contracts date back to Biblical times. The roots of the modern day futures contract started in the Midwest in the 1800s. It was there that grain traders faced volatile market conditions, which ultimately led to the creation of a futures exchange.

Chicago, just by coincidence, was strategically located. It was central to the grain farmers and also situated at the base of Lake Michigan — one of the five Great Lakes in North America. Easy access to the Great Lakes made shipping easier, and the farmers and grain traders found it convenient to meet in Chicago and exchange commodities through agreements called "to arrive" contracts. In

1848, merchants formed the Chicago Board of Trade (CBOT), the first and still the largest futures exchange in the world today.

Another exchange formed quite a while later, in 1874, and was named the Chicago Produce Exchange, which traded mainly butter, eggs, poultry, and other perishable agricultural products. The butter and egg traders withdrew from this exchange to form their own exchange called the Butter and Egg Board. In 1919, the Butter and Egg Board was reorganized to provide a futures market and was renamed the Chicago Mercantile Exchange (CME).

Today, the CBOT and CME are two of the primary exchanges for many commodity and financial futures contracts, although there are many other exchanges including:

- Kansas City Board of Trade (KCBT)
- MidAmerica Commodity Exchange (Mid Am). This is technically owned by the CBOT but operates independently.
- Minneapolis Grain Exchange (MGE)
- New York Board of Trade (NYBOT)
- Philadelphia Board of Trade (PBOT)
- New York Cotton Exchange (CTN/NYCE)
- New York Mercantile Exchange/COMEX (NYMEX/COMEX)
- Twin Cities Board of Trade (TCBT)
- Winnipeg Commodity Exchange (WCE)

You can buy futures contracts covering many different categories including:

- Agricultural (e.g., corn, soybeans, and lean hog)
- Metals (e.g., gold, silver)
- Chemicals (e.g., benzene and mixed xylenes)
- Interest rate/financial (e.g., eurodollars, Treasury bonds)
- Forest products (e.g., lumber)
- Indexes (e.g., S&P 500, Nasdaq 100)
- Currencies (e.g., Australian dollar, Brazilian real)
- Weather (e.g., heating degree day, cooling degree day)

Hopefully you're starting to see that futures contracts have a beneficial role in society and just may be an asset to your investment portfolio as well. They provide an efficient means to transfer risk from one party to another. In the car example, the dealer was concerned with falling prices and a lost sale while you were concerned with rising prices and the possibility of never finding the car. By using the futures contract, you each transferred your fears (risks) to the other party — and both you and the car dealer considered it a good deal.

These are motivating reasons why futures markets were created. They provide a means for providing more liquidity and thus lower prices. The fact that there are some speculators willing to gamble on some trades for a profit is irrelevant. The risk the speculators take is voluntary and should not be considered a negative aspect of the futures markets. Speculators, as we will soon see, are also beneficial as they provide a larger supply of buyers and sellers, which creates narrower spreads (the difference between the bid and ask prices) on the prices of futures contracts. Because there are speculators willing to gamble on price movements, manufacturers are able to reduce their risk and create products for less money. Hopefully you now understand the naivete of those who claim that futures markets are nothing more than a forum for legalized gambling.

I Don't Need Pork Bellies, so Why Do I Need to Understand Futures?

In October of 1997, futures contracts began trading on the Dow Jones Industrial Averages as a precursor to the SSFs on equities (individual stocks). Single-stock futures are expected to begin trading by the end of 2002. That's right; soon you'll be able to buy or sell futures contracts on many of your favorite publicly traded companies. So while you may not have a desire to invest in pork bellies or other obscure commodities, futures contracts will play an increasingly important role for your stock portfolio in the coming years.

It will pay to understand them.

Hedgers, Speculators and Arbitrageurs

We've shown how beneficial futures contracts can be, so why all the hype about risk with futures contracts? The more accurate way to talk about risk with futures is to say they *can* be risky rather than to say they *are* risky.

The reason why is that there are two main parties involved with most futures contracts: *hedgers* and *speculators.* The hedgers are those who are trying to avoid risk and transfer it to another party. In most cases, the other party is a *speculator* — someone who actively seeks risk to make a profit. Speculators are willing to expose themselves to price risk because they expect to profit from price movements. Unfortunately, it is the speculators who you read about in the newspaper and who give futures markets their risky reputation.

There's a good reason you don't read about hedgers in the news. They make boring stories, which is certainly not good for the journalists. Think about which of the following hypothetical headlines would make you buy a newspaper:

- *Quaker Oats protects their oat supply through futures markets*
- *Historic Baring's Bank bankrupt by rogue gambler in the futures markets*

Both stories used futures contracts. Both parties took their respective positions along with their respective risks, yet only one story will be heard. Futures markets can be risky if used thoughtlessly.

Technically, there is a third party involved in the functioning of the futures markets known as *arbitrageurs.* Arbitrageurs are those who look for "free money" lying around in the market. When we say free money, we really mean a guaranteed profit for no cash outlay. Many people incorrectly believe that an arbitrage profit is simple a guaranteed profit, but that is only partly correct. If this second condition of "no cash outlay" is not met, the purchase of a government bond qualifies as arbitrage because a profit is guaranteed. However, the government bond requires a cash outlay for a specific period of time before the profit is realized.

The classic example of arbitrage is where a stock trader may see shares of IBM asking $125 on the American Exchange and bidding $125.10 on the New York Stock Exchange. The arbitrageur could buy them on the American and immediately sell them on the New York for an immediate 10-cent profit. These actions will put buying pressure on the American Exchange, and selling pressure on the New York and will continue until IBM is priced the same on both exchanges. While this may not sound like a big profit, bear in mind that large institutions often carry out arbitrage in large block trades and the profits can quickly add up. It is very big business. In fact, in the early 1990s there was a Japanese firm that paid $23 million dollars in order to gain one second quicker access time to currency quotes for the purpose of arbitrage.

While arbitrage may sound like the ideal way to invest, it is unfortunately nearly impossible for retail investors mainly due to speed of executions and commissions. Large institutions have traders on the floors that actively seek out these opportunities and pay a very small processing fee to do so. In fact, you may have seen the strange hand signals that are used on the floors of futures exchanges to designate the orders. These signals basically evolved from the arbitrageurs. When traders saw a trade in one pit on the exchange and needed another trade in another pit across the room, it was much easier to flash a hand signal to that pit to complete the trade. Otherwise, by the time they walked over to it the opportunity often was already gone.

The word arbitrage is derived from the French word *arbitrer*, meaning to judge. Arbitrageurs are "judging" the values between two assets and profiting from any discrepancies. Many incorrectly feel that this should be illegal as if these arbitrageurs are cheating the markets. However, arbitrageurs are actually performing an important economic function by ensuring that prices are, in fact, fair for everybody. If one asset is *relatively* too cheap, you can be assured that arbitrageurs will come to the rescue and bid its price up. Likewise, if one should become *relatively* too expensive, arbitrageurs will quickly sell it and bring the price down. We'll talk more about arbitrageurs in Chapter 4 and take a closer look at how they provide a very important economic function.

So while you will likely never participate in an arbitrage trade, just be aware that they occur throughout every day to keep futures prices from getting out of line from where they should be trading in relation to their underlying assets.

Okay, Get Rid of the Speculators and Then I'll Invest in the Futures Markets!

So you think it's the speculators who are to blame for all the risk, right? Well, not exactly. Without the speculators, you have no futures market. Speculators are essential for providing liquidity (lots of willing buyers and sellers), which helps to keep narrow spreads between bid and ask prices. When there are many speculative sellers available, prices tend to be lower, which is good for the conservative buyer. Likewise, when there are many speculative buyers, prices tend to be higher, which is good for the conservative seller.

Speculators are necessary for any well-functioning market, not just the futures markets. You may be thinking, "None of those speculative markets are for me; I'm sticking with my conservative bonds." Well think about who is on the other side of that conservative bond trade of yours. It's a speculator. It is someone who thinks they can make more money by borrowing from you at one rate and creating something of value that yields a higher rate. Without high-risk speculators, the conservative bond market would cease to exist.

Speculators should actually be welcomed members of the markets. If you are selling any asset, say shares of stock, should it matter to you if the buyer is going to conservatively lock them up in a safe deposit box for 10 years or recklessly gamble and try to flip them for a 1/4-point profit? Obviously, it shouldn't matter. A buyer is a buyer and the more buyers there are, the more competitive the prices become, which is great for you as a seller. So don't fall prey to the belief of the financial press, which often claims that speculators destroy the financial markets. Speculators are an absolute necessity for financial markets to operate — and they occasionally make interesting headlines as well!

We've covered the basics of futures markets and you should now see the potential for managing risks of your financial portfolio. Let's take the next step and see in detail how a futures contract actually works.

How Do Futures Contracts Work?

One of the problems in understanding futures contracts for new investors is that they deal with commodities that are foreign to us. They may deal in pork bellies, soybeans, euros, mixed xylenes, or the De Witt Benzene Index. Right away we feel confused and think the concept is a lot harder to understand than it really is.

For starters, let's use a simple example that's the equivalent of a futures contract. This will help to reinforce the mechanics of how and why a futures contract works. Once you understand the basic motions, understanding a real futures contract will be easy.

A Very Simple Example of a Futures Contract

Let's say I have a digital camera that is worth $500 — that's the amount I could quickly sell it for in a few days. I will need $500 three months from now, and I'm willing to sell my camera to generate the cash. Because digital cameras are relatively new, there are many new competitors entering the market, which may drive price down. At the same time, new technology is quickly making the cameras better, which allows for manufacturers to charge more for them. If prices move higher, the prices of used cameras will rise right along with them. Therefore, we're uncertain about what will happen with prices and we could experience sizeable price swings.

Because I need the money in three months, there is a risk that I may not be able to get $500 for it at that time. While it is possible I may get more, my concern is that I could get less. I would be very interested in finding a way to guard against this risk.

Let's say my friend wants to buy a similar camera but will not have the money for three months. He's willing to pay $500 for it and I'm willing to accept that offer. However, we cannot close the deal because he does not have the money today. If he waits for three months to buy the camera, he faces the risk of rising prices. While I am interested in guarding against falling prices, he is interested in guarding against rising prices.

When one guards against risk with financial assets, it is called a hedge. I need a hedge against falling prices and my friend needs a hedge against rising prices. A hedge is an asset whose value will move in the opposite direction as that of the asset you're trying to protect. In other words, if the price of the asset you're trying to protect falls, the price of the hedge will rise. An asset used as a hedge is usually not intended to make money but only to offset losses.

Insurance on your home is a hedge. If you buy insurance, the value of that policy declines as the year goes on assuming you make no claims. However, if you have $20,000 worth of hurricane damage, your policy — your hedge — now pays you $20,000. Notice how you do not profit from the hedge since you lost $20,000 and gained that same amount. Hedges just offset losses.

Is there a way my friend and I can create a hedge to address each of our concerns of rising and falling prices respectively?

Yes there is. The two of us can hedge our respective risks by entering into an agreement (a contract) to sell and buy the camera for $500 in three months (the future). That's all a futures contract is (remember, this would technically be a forward agreement since it is a private arrangement and not traded on an exchange, but the concept is exactly the same). To make things a little more interesting, let's say I live in Florida and my friend lives in California.

Three months go by and it is time to make the deal. Prices, however, have risen and similar used cameras are now selling for $650. My friend definitely wants to buy mine at the agreed upon price of $500 because of the recent increase in prices. While I may not be so happy about selling it, I am under contract to do so.[1]

---

[1] If I back away from the contract, then my friend is faced with default risk. This is the risk we talked about earlier and is a significant risk of forward contracts. It is default risk that the clearing firms guard against and is the reason why using standardized contracts is a financially practical concept, despite some of their shortcomings.

There are a couple of ways we can settle this. One method is straightforward; I can ship the camera worth $650 to him and receive a $500 check in exchange. If so, the terms of the contract are satisfied and the contract is executed. I lose a $650 camera and gain a $500 check. My friend has the opposite set of transactions and gains the camera but loses the check. The net effect is that I'm out $150 and he gains by that amount. Figure 1.2 shows the effects on both of us if I ship the camera.

Method #1: Ship the camera	
My perspective	**Friend's perspective**
-$650 camera	-$650 camera
+$500 check	-$500 check
-$150	+$150

Figure 1.2

If I ship the camera to him, I have a lost opportunity of $150. That means had I *not* entered the contract with my friend, I could now sell my camera for $650, which would put another $150 in my pocket. But because I did enter the contract, I must ship the $650 camera and receive a $500 check for it. I will not realize the additional $150 of market value.

But let's look at another way to settle the contract. If my friend could buy a similar camera in California for $650, couldn't we call it even if I just send him a check for $150 to make up his loss from the $500 agreed upon price? That way I don't have to ship the camera and he doesn't face the cost or risk of damage during shipping. He buys the camera in his area through a local dealer for $650 but receives my check for $150 and effectively pays $500, which is the price we agreed upon three months ago. His $500 plus my $150 check nets him the $650 he needs to buy the camera at current market prices. He gets his camera for the contractual $500 and I'm out $150 regardless of whether I ship the camera or just send him a check.

In this second method of settlement, we could say I paid him $150 so I could get out of the contract. I have effectively purchased the contract back from him, and it is now considered complete. Notice that when I purchased the contract from him, I got out of the contract, so I am no longer obligated by its terms and do not need to ship the camera. Figure 1.3 shows the effects of this second method of settlement on each of us:

Method #2: Close out for cash	
My perspective	**Friend's perspective**
-$150 check	+$150 check
+$650 camera proceeds	-$650 camera proceeds
+$500	-$500

Figure 1.3

If I spend $150 cash, I get to keep the camera worth $650. Because I had to spend that money in order to keep the camera, its value has effectively been lowered to $500. My friend now must spend $650 for a camera but receives a $150 check from me, which effectively lowers his purchase price to $500. Notice that I am left with a camera worth $500 (which I can sell locally), but my effective selling price is $500, which is exactly how I wanted to end up three months ago.

Compare Figures 1.1 and 1.3. In the first scenario the net effect was that I lost $150 of value, but in the second scenario I lost $150 cash. I also received $500 cash with the first method but received that same amount of value in the second. The bottom line is that either method effectively makes the purchase price paid by my friend and sales price received by me the same — $500. Although I never ship the camera in method #2, I effectively transferred its gain in value to my friend.

We have just seen two methods in fulfilling the contract if prices rise. Let's look at how we could complete the contract if prices fell instead.

Let's assume that after three months, similar cameras are selling for $300 instead of $650. While my friend certainly isn't interested in paying $500 for mine, he is under contractual obligation to do so. The first method of settlement is to execute the contract and ship the camera worth $300 and receive a $500 check from him. In that case, I have an effective gain of $200 at his expense since I am selling an asset for $500 that is only worth $300.

Figure 1.4 shows that shipping the camera causes me to lose a $300 camera but gain a $500 check, which was the agreed upon price. This nets me a $200 gain. Likewise, my friend is exposed to the opposite set of transactions and receives a $300 camera but spends $500 cash for a $200 loss.

Method #1: Ship the camera	
My perspective	**Friend's perspective**
-$300 camera	+$300 camera
+$500 check	-$500 check
+$200	-$200

Figure 1.4

But once again, rather than taking the time, cost, and risk to ship the camera, he could buy the camera in California for only $300 and send me a check for $200. This effectively makes him pay the agreed upon price of $500 for the camera. I could then sell my camera for $300 in Florida plus gain his $200 check, which nets me the $500 agreed upon price. Whether I ship the camera or accept his $200 check, he effectively pays $500 to obtain a camera and I sell mine for $500, which is exactly how we wanted to end up three months ago.

So our second method of completing this agreement is that he buys back the contract from me for $200 as shown in Figure1.5:

Method #2: Close out for cash	
My perspective	**Friend's perspective**
+$300 camera proceeds	-$300 camera
+$200 check	-$200 check
+$500	-$500

Figure 1.5

The most important point to understand is that whether prices rise or fall and regardless of the method we choose to settle the contract, I receive $500 for my camera and my friend spends $500 to gain a camera. Our fears of rising or falling prices are perfectly hedged by simply entering into an agreement to prearrange these transactions three months earlier.

If we ship the camera, Figures 1.2 and 1.4 show that I actually receive a $500 check from my friend. However, if we choose to not ship the camera, Figures 1.3 and 1.5 show that I gain $500 in value and my friend loses $500 in value. I either get a $500 check for certain or $500 in value for certain, which is exactly what I wanted three months earlier. My friend either spends $500 for the camera or spends $500 in value to gain a camera, which is exactly what he wanted at the onset of the contract.

In about 95% of the actual futures contracts, investors just offset their obligations by closing the contract out for cash and "offsetting" the contract, thus causing it to be closed. Investors and speculators just close out their positions by either paying or receiving money, which mathematically makes it equivalent to their buying and selling prices to which they agreed at the start of the contract.

Notice how easy it would be for an untrained eye to see my $150 "loss" when camera prices rose and my friend's $200 "loss" when prices fell and thus view this futures contract as a speculative, risky arrangement! But a close examination reveals that's not the case. Three months earlier when I wanted to sell my camera, I was concerned that I may get less than $500 for it. If I can sell my camera for $650, then I do not see sending somebody else a check for $150 as a loss. I am perfectly willing to do that. My concern of a lower price was perfectly hedged by the contract. Likewise, my friend was concerned with paying more than $500 to gain a camera in three months. He's perfectly willing to send a check if he's able to pick up the camera in three months for less money. His worry about paying more for the camera was perfectly hedged by the contract. Futures contracts allow people to hedge risks of rising or falling prices. In most cases, money just changes hands and the underlying assets are never delivered.

In some futures contracts, you couldn't even take delivery if you wanted to. Rather, the contracts are cash settled but, as we've seen, there's really no difference in the two methods. Cash-settled futures most often occur with indices such as the S&P 500 or the Nasdaq 100. Rather than delivering every stock in the index which would be rather burdensome, that contract only settles in cash.

A Futures Contract Is a Zero-Sum Game

We said that hedges are not intended to provide profits but rather offset losses. Just as with the home insurance example, the home-owner gained a $20,000 check but lost $20,000 in value of the home, which is a net breakeven. Any arrangement that operates where one person's gain is exactly another person's loss is called a zero-sum game. A zero-sum game just means that one person cannot be made better off without making another equally worse off.

A futures contract is a zero-sum game. This simply means that, in the end, no new money is brought to market such as when new shares of stock are issued. Futures contracts do not provide a means to raise new capital, which is often one of their criticisms. In the camera example, when prices rose $150, I lost that amount and my friend gained that amount. Likewise, when prices fell $200, I gained that amount and he lost that amount for a net zero gain or loss in the market. Keep this in mind as you hear about the "devastating" losses created in the futures markets. There is always a party on the other side of the trade who profited by that exact amount. So the futures markets do not create disastrous "holes" in the financial system, but rather allow hedgers and speculators to hedge risks by simply passing money from one to another. Those "holes" are filled by gains of equal size.

Long and Short Positions

In financial lingo, if you own an asset (stock, bond, futures contract, etc.) you are long the position. With a long position, you are hoping to profit from an increase in that asset's price. You are attempting to "buy low, sell high." However, it is also possible to profit from a decrease in the asset's price. To do so you must reverse the transactions by selling the asset first and then buying it back later at hopefully a lower price. If you sell first, you are "short" the position. Short sellers attempt to "sell high, buy low." While it may sound complicated, short sales can be accomplished with relatively the same quickness and ease as purchasing a stock from your broker.

Short selling was even demonstrated in the comedy hit movie *Trading Places* with Eddie Murphy and Dan Aykroyd when the two were selling frozen concentrated orange juice futures contracts to get even with their heartless bosses. The bosses see the two down on the trading floor when one asks, "What are they doing down there?" The other suddenly realizes what's happening and replies, "They're selling, Mortimer!" After the crop report is released, the futures prices plunge and you see Eddie and Dan buying back the contracts (wearing big smiles).

If you want more details on the mechanics of short selling for stocks, you can read more about it in the appendix at the end of this chapter. *For now, just understand that long positions make money if prices rise, and short positions make money if prices fall.*

Many investors who are new to futures get easily confused when they're trying to decide if the hedger or speculator should buy or sell the futures contract. In other words, should they be the long contract or the short one? If you are speculating, the answer is easy and is no different from stocks, bonds, options, or other assets. If the think the price will rise, you buy the futures contract. If you think prices will fall, you short the contract. Where it gets tricky for some is when you consider a hedging transaction, such as when my friend and I wanted to hedge against rising and falling camera prices respectively. It's actually very easy to figure out and there are a couple of ways to do it that you may find helpful.

First, I was afraid of falling prices. How can I protect myself? Obviously I need an asset that rises in price as prices fall — I need a short hedge. If I sell (short) the contract, I can protect myself from falling prices since the short contract will rise in price if the underlying prices fall.

My friend, on the other hand, was afraid of rising prices. He needs a long hedge for price protection. If he buys the contract, it will rise in price and offset his costs in the future if underlying prices should rise.

Because I needed a short hedge and my friend needed a long hedge, we were able to match up our needs and create a "futures" contract. He would be the buyer of the contract and I would be the seller.

Key points:

You <u>buy a futures contract</u> (long position) if you wish to hedge against <u>rising</u> prices in the future.

You <u>sell a futures contract</u> (short position) if you wish to hedge against <u>falling</u> prices in the future.

If you are not comfortable thinking in terms of long and short hedges, you can use another method, possibly more straightforward, to determine who should be long and short the contract.

Since I would be the <u>seller</u> of the camera in the future, I will need to be the <u>seller</u> (short position) of the contract. Similarly, my friend will be the <u>buyer</u> of the camera in the future so he would be a <u>buyer</u> (long position) of the contract. Just remember that a buyer is a buyer and a seller is a seller. Buying a futures contract is the same as buying something in the future. Selling a futures contract is the same as selling something in the future. It's not any more difficult than that.

Key points:

You <u>buy a futures contract</u> if you are willing to <u>buy</u> the underlying asset in the future.

You <u>sell a futures contract</u> if you are willing to <u>sell</u> the underlying asset in the future.

Refer back to Figures 1.3 and 1.5 for a moment. In Figure 1.3 we said that I could close out the contract by paying $150 to my friend. Now it should make more sense as to why that worked. He was the long position and I was the short position. Because prices rose, my short position was hurt by $150 dollars (remember, short positions profit if prices fall) so I can pay him that amount and the contract is considered complete. Notice it is the loser who pays the winner.

Likewise in Figure 1.5 we assumed that prices fell by $200. In that case, my friend would have to pay me $200 to close out the position. That's because his long position was hurt by the fall in price and my short position was strengthened, and the loser must pay the winner.

Notice that this contract was closed for equal gains and losses at the same time. In other words, if I wish to end the contract, I have to rely on my friend to take the opposing side and close it out, too. What if that person does not wish to do so at that time? In the real world of futures trading, it does not matter what the other person wishes to do. Because futures contracts are standardized, I would only need to buy the contract from another seller. In effect, I will have switched places with that person and he becomes the new short position paired with my friend. Likewise, if my friend wishes to close out the contract, he does not need me to agree to it. He simply sells the contract to another buyer. If so, that new buyer is now the new long position and I am still the short position. The ability to swap contracts like this, to allow buyers and sellers a way out at their discretion, is perhaps the biggest advantage of standardized contracts.

For every futures contract there must be one buyer (long position) and one seller (short position), which is why a futures contract is a zero-sum game. Any gain in the long positions is canceled out by equal losses in the short positions. This is not true for the stock market. While there are usually some short positions for any given stock, it is not a necessary condition. It is therefore possible for all stockholders to have a profit on a given day. If Intel rises $1 and there are no short positions, then all stockholders have increased their wealth by $1 per share. If this happens in the futures markets, then half the positions have a gain and half have a loss.

This camera example represents the very essence of any futures contract. If you understand what took place with the different scenarios of rising and falling prices, you will be able to follow the more obscure commodities with a real futures contract. Then you'll be prepared to understand how these assets can be used to improve your performance in the stock market once single-stock futures are introduced. Let's now run through an example of a real futures contract and see how they can be used to hedge day-to-day business risks.

Understanding a Real Futures Contract

Now that we understand the basic mechanics of how a futures contract works, we can apply that same reasoning to a real contract and it will be much easier to comprehend.

We said that there are many types of futures contracts, and currencies are certainly one of the more popular contracts for businesses involved in importing and exporting. These firms face *exchange rate risk*, and it can be a serious threat to firms in this industry. If a U.S. firm is going to accept payment in a foreign currency in the future, they must exchange that foreign currency for U.S. dollars at some time. The risk lies in the fact that the exchange rate at that time may be unfavorable and large losses could develop. Let's stick with our car dealer from Chapter 1 and see how he could use futures contracts to hedge the considerable risk of currency fluctuations.

Assume that the U.S. Lexus dealer is going to order 20 Lexus convertibles. The cars will be built in Japan and shipped to the U.S. in three months. At that time, the car dealer must pay 125,000,000 yen (¥125,000,000) for delivery.

How much is ¥125,000,000 worth in U.S. dollars? That depends on the exchange rate between the two currencies. Let's assume the current exchange rate is $1 = ¥125, which is how you will likely see quotes in your local newspaper. That just means that $1 can be exchanged for 125 yen. These quotes are called the *spot* rate since money can be exchanged "on the spot," or immediately, at that rate.[2] If the car dealer needed to buy the cars today, he would need to pay ¥125,000,000/125 = $1,000,000 for the shipment. In other words, one million U.S. dollars will purchase 125 million Japanese yen, which is the current amount needed to fulfill the contract price.

In order to hedge the risk of rising yen prices, the dealer could buy the yen today. However, as with any payment, the car dealer does not want to pay for something that is not due immediately so

---

[2] Although the spot market is considered "immediate" delivery, it is technically a two-day settlement.

that the dealership may earn interest on the money in the meantime. Rather than buying the yen today, the dealer could wait for three months and buy them at that time. Of course, the risk of waiting for three months to pass before buying the Japanese yen is that the yen may be much more expensive at that time, which means the cars would cost significantly more than one million dollars. So what can the car dealer do? Just as our camera example showed how we could guard against rising prices of a camera, we can use the same principles, on a much bigger scale, to guard against rising prices of Japanese yen. The car dealer simply needs to prearrange the purchase of yen three months into the future.

Remember what we learned earlier regarding long and short hedges. Our car dealer is afraid of <u>rising</u> yen prices, so he will need a <u>long</u> contract in order to hedge that fear — he will need to buy a Japanese yen futures contract today, thus locking in his future purchase price of yen. Using our alternative method to determine whether he should be long or short is that the car dealer is a <u>buyer</u> of yen in the future so he will be a <u>buyer</u> of the yen contract. Before we can understand how a futures contract works with currencies, we need to understand some basic notations about reading currency quotes.

A Brief Detour: Understanding Currency Quotes

We assumed that the current exchange rate is $1 = ¥125, which is known as an indirect quote or foreign quote. An *indirect* quote uses one unit of the local currency (in this case, $1) and then allows the *foreign* currency to float. It answers the question, "How many units of foreign currency can I get with one unit of my home currency?"

Sometimes you will see exchange rates listed from the viewpoint of the home country, which is called a direct quote (if the home currency is the U.S.). A direct quote is listed as one unit of the foreign currency and allows the home currency to float. It answers the question, "How many dollars does it take to buy one unit of the foreign currency?" If the indirect quote is $1 = ¥125, the direct quote will be the reciprocal amount, which is 1/125 or ¥1 = $.008. Notice how the yen is fixed at one unit and the home currency is allowed to float.

It is important to understand these two methods of quoting, since most (not all) currency contracts are quoted in direct terms. If you do not understand how to read the quotes then you will not know at what price you are agreeing to buy or sell in the future. To reduce the risk of rising yen prices (falling dollar), the car dealer can enter into a futures contract to <u>buy</u> Japanese yen in three months.

Earlier we said that futures contracts are standardized as to size, quality, delivery and other aspects. It just so happens that the size of the Japanese yen contract is fixed at 12,500,000 yen. If the dealer buys a yen futures contract, he will be purchasing that many yen in three months. Assume it is now December, which means the car dealer will need to buy the March Japanese yen futures contract (three months ahead), which is currently quoting 7850. What does this quote mean? Remember we said that most currency contracts are quoted in direct terms, and the yen is no exception. However, because the value of the dollar to the yen is so strong, there's a little twist to the way quotes on the yen are displayed. A quote of 7850 is really the direct quote without the front two zeros, which means ¥1 = $.007850. If the car dealer buys one March contract, he will lock himself into a payment of 12,500,000 * $.007850 = $98,125 in three months.

On a technical note, the Japanese yen futures are really quoted in points with one point being equal to one millionth of a dollar, which is $.000001 or $1/1,000,000 per Japanese yen. A quote of 7850 points is equal to 7850/1,000,000, which equals $.007850 per yen and is exactly the same answer we arrived at previously. Whenever you see a quote on the Japanese yen, simply divide that quote by 1 million and that's how many dollars you're agreeing to pay per yen.

Now back to our car dealer's problem. He has a guaranteed delivery of 20 cars in three months with a fixed payment of ¥125,000,000, which is *anticipated* to be valued at $1 million since the current exchange rate is $1 = ¥125 (or $.008 per yen). It is the uncertainty of the future value of the yen that he wishes to hedge. If the price of the yen rises, the dealer may end up with a much larger than anticipated expense.

He can do one of two things: One, he can pay the current rate for the Japanese yen and pay $.008 dollars per yen and hold onto the yen for three months. In order to do this, the car dealer will miss out on the interest that could be earned on $1 million over three months. It is possible the dealer may hold the yen in a Japanese bank to earn interest, but there may be differences in interest rates and the dealer would need an account at a Japanese bank, which may be more trouble than it's worth.

His second option is to enter into the futures contract and pay .007850 dollars per yen in three months. On the surface it certainly seems like the dealer should enter into the futures contract since he can delay the payment *and* get a more favorable exchange rate. Remember, the current yen price is $.008 for spot delivery but the dealer can enter into a futures contract and purchase them for .007850, which is a little cheaper, in three months.

Price Discovery

In this case, the markets are signaling that they expect the dollar to strengthen against the yen over the next three months; that's why it will take fewer dollars to buy one yen in three months (.007850 versus .008). This is yet another benefit of futures markets. They provide a forum for price discovery — a way to collect opinions of market participants as to the direction of prices. Futures markets provide the forum to bring all the bids and offers together in one centralized location, which gives you the market consensus of direction by simply glancing at the quotes.

Normally, if most people were asked for an opinion as to whether the dollar would strengthen or weaken against the yen, they would be lost for an answer. With futures markets, the answer is easy and you simply look at the quotes — that's price discovery. In Chapter 4 you'll see that there are some markets where price discovery works better than others, but for now just be aware that futures markets provide this very important economic function.

The markets are signaling for a decrease in the price of yen relative to the dollar, so this actually opens up a third choice for the dealer. He may elect to use this information, simply wait for three months to pass and then make payment at that time for *hopefully* a more favorable rate. Just because the markets are signaling for a decrease, though, does not mean it will happen. Because the dealer is really concerned with the yen rising against the dollar, entering into the futures contract seems to be his best course of action. Of course, by entering into the March yen contract and locking in a rate of $.007850 per yen today, the dealer runs another type of risk in that the exchange rate may be even cheaper after three months. This is the same type of risk my friend was exposed to when buying the camera in Chapter 1. But futures contracts are not used to determine the optimal price; they are used to lock in costs and profits. The dealer's concern is that yen prices will rise; by entering into the futures contract, he can eliminate this fear.

Because he will pay ¥125,000,000 in three months and each contract is for 12,500,000 yen, he will need to buy 125,000,000/12,500,000 = 10 futures contracts on the yen. In most real-life cases, the number of required contracts will not work out this evenly; this was done intentionally to make the example easier to follow. But for now, just understand that many times the hedger will need to slightly under- or over-hedge, which is another drawback with standardized contracts. For example, if the payment for the cars were ¥115,000,000, he would need to buy 115,000,000/12,500,000 = 9.2 contracts. If he only buys 9 he is a little under-hedged, and he's overhedged if he buys 10. If he could find someone to take the other side of the trade for him, he could enter into a forward agreement for exactly ¥115,000,000 and be perfectly hedged. Once again, finding this other person can be difficult to say the least. If the dealer does find someone, he must have an attorney draw up the contracts and, well, you get the idea. It's not easy. The futures contracts can be executed in seconds and the clearing corporation guarantees its fulfillment. Sometimes being a little under- or over-hedged is worth it. Let's look at how the futures contract manages the risk for our car dealer under various scenarios.

Scenario #1: The Yen Falls

Let's assume that the yen does in fact fall relative to the dollar (which is predicted by the market through price discovery) to an exchange rate of $.007840 in March. If this is the case, the futures contract will be trading for very close to the spot rate, quoting 7840. The reason it must be quoting close to the spot rate is because the futures contract will almost be expired and is virtually the same as the spot rate. You'll see a more formal arbitrage argument shortly.

We know that in March the dealer was expecting a cash payment of 125,000,000 * $.007850 = $981,250 so let's see what he could do in this scenario.

With the yen trading lower, the dealer has two choices: He can use the futures contract and pay .007850 per yen, or can close out the futures contract and buy yen in the open market.

Just as with our camera example, we will soon see that it doesn't really matter which choice the dealer makes; both result in the same outcome. We'll step through both choices to explain why it makes no difference.

Choice #1: Yen falls. Dealer <u>does not</u> use his March futures contract:

Because the yen has fallen, the dealer may decide to not use the futures contract and will prefer to just purchase the 125,000,000 yen in the open market for the cheaper price of $.007840 or a total purchase price of $980,000. The dealer was locked into a purchase price, though, of $981,250 so he appears to be ahead by $1,250 by not using the futures contract. However, in order to get out of his futures contract, he must enter an *offsetting* position, which means he will have to sell the same contract as the one he is long. The March contract can currently be sold for the spot price of 7840. Because he agreed to pay 7850, this results in a loss of (.007850-.007840) * 125,000,000 = $1,250.

So even though the dealer appeared to be saving $1,250 by purchasing yen in the open market and not using the futures contract, it is only an illusion. He must pay that amount to get out of the futures contract. Remember, futures are not options so the dealer has an obligation to fulfill the contract unless he enters an offsetting futures position.

The dealer was ahead by $1,250 by purchasing yen in the open market and not using the futures contract; however, he lost $1,250 in closing out the contract for a net wash. This net wash situation will be true for any Japanese yen quote below the contract price of 7850 — the loss on the futures will equal the gain in using the spot market.

However, had the dealer not entered the futures market back in December, he would be ahead by $1,250. An unsuspecting eye sees that using the futures contract resulted in a speculative loss of $1,250. It does *not* see that the dealer is also ahead by that amount by using the spot market; *nor* does it see that the dealer would be ahead had the yen risen against the dollar, which was his main reason for entering into the futures contract.

Choice #2: Yen falls. Dealer <u>uses</u> his March futures contract:

The dealer could elect to use the futures contract and take delivery of 125,000,000 yen at a price of $.007850 for a total payment of $981,250. If so, he is overpaying by $1,250 by not using the spot market where yen can be purchased for $.007840 per yen or $980,000; however, he does not take a $1,250 loss on the futures contract either.

We can see that it makes no difference, mathematically, whether or not the dealer uses the futures contract to purchase the yen. However, no matter which choice he makes, there is a $1,250 loss when compared to the alternative choice three months earlier of not entering the contract at all. Had the dealer not entered the futures market back in December, he would be ahead by $1,250. Using the futures contract "cost" him an additional $1,250. Keep in mind, though, that the purpose of using the futures was not to protect against falling prices but rather against rising prices.

Even though the futures contract appears to be a loser in this case, you have to remember that the dealer would have paid $1,000,000 back in December to insure (hedge) delivery for March. The dealer hardly sees his payment of $981,250 as a loss. That's the price he agreed to pay back in December. He's more than happy to pay $1,250 to close out the futures contract at a "loss" in order to save $1,250 in the spot market. Remember, these "gains" and "losses" in the futures contract just mathematically ensure that both the buyer and seller are locked into their original agreed upon prices. The dealer pays $980,000 in the spot market and incurs a loss of $1,250 on the futures contract for a total cost of $981,250 — the original price he agree to pay.

Scenario #2: The Yen Rises

Even though the market was predicting a fall in the value of the yen, this obviously does not mean the yen must fall. That is just a market consensus and, while the information is valuable, it is not always correct. Let's assume now that an unforeseen event happens and the yen rises to an exchange rate of $1 = ¥126.50 or ¥1 = $.007905. If so, the Japanese yen contract will be trading for (or very close to) the spot price of 7905.

Once again, the car dealer has two choices; and either choice will result in the same outcome.

Choice 1: Yen rises. Dealer <u>does not</u> use his March futures contract:
With the yen trading at $.007905, the dealer can buy yen in the market for a total payment of 125,000,000 * .007905 = $988,125. However, in order to not use his futures contract he must close it out in the open market by selling the equivalent contract, which will be trading for 7905. He was under contract to pay 7850 but can sell that same contract for 7905, which is a gain of .007905 - .007850 = .000055 * 125,000,000 = $6,875. In effect, the dealer pays $988,125 in the spot market but also receives a gain of $6,875 from the sale of the futures for a net payment of $981,250, the price he *expected* to pay when he initiated the futures position back in December. Had the dealer not entered the futures contract then, he would be exposed to an unexpected $6,875 expense in March. By entering the futures contract, the dealer has controlled costs and is ahead by $6,875.

Choice 2: Yen rises. Dealer <u>uses</u> his March futures contract:
Because the yen is trading higher than his contract price of 7850, the car dealer could decide to use the contract to purchase the yen. If so, his payment will be $.007850 * 125,000,000 = $981,000, a savings of $6,875 as compared to using the spot market. A net gain will result for any spot price above $.007850 in March.

This savings of $6,875 is exactly the amount of the gain in the futures contract when the dealer opted to not use the contract in Choice #1. If he uses the contract to purchase the yen, he cannot sell it for an equal gain either. Whether or not the dealer uses the futures contract, he is hedged against any *increase* in the price of yen through March — this is the reason he entered the futures contract.

Because it doesn't make a difference to the dealer whether or not he uses the contract, as stated before, most users of futures contracts will just close out the futures contract at either a gain or loss and then purchase or sell the underlying asset in the spot market.

Why not use the contract? There are specific guidelines for taking delivery of the underlying asset. Contrary to what you've probably heard, nobody is going to pull up in front of your house and dump a bunch of cattle on your front lawn. In fact, the CME rulebook describes approved stockyards for live cattle as follows:

CME Approved Stockyards

Deliveries on exchange contracts of live beef cattle, feeder cattle, and lean hogs can be made only from public livestock yards designated and approved for delivery by the Exchange.

A public livestock yard shall not be eligible for deliveries as an approved stockyard unless it is a stockyard within the definition of the Packers and Stockyards Act (Ch. 9 United States Code, Sections 181-3, 201-217a and 221-9) and has received notice to that effect from the Secretary of Agriculture. Approved stockyards shall be required to keep such records, make such reports and be subject to inspection and regulation by the Secretary of Agriculture, as provided in said Packers and Stockyards Act.

Rather than dealing with the headaches of filing delivery forms and other specific formalities for taking delivery, most hedgers will close out the contracts in the open market and then deal with their own suppliers on a local level. The important point to understand is that whether or not the dealer uses the contract, there are advantages and disadvantages, and the net gains or losses to the car dealer are zero. These are summarized in Figure 1.6:

	Yen Falls		Yen Rises	
	Advantage	**Disadvantage**	**Advantage**	**Disadvantage**
Uses contract	Does not take loss on futures contract	Takes equal loss by paying more for Yen with contract	Pays less for Yen by using contract	Loses equal gain by not selling contract
Does not use contract	Pays less for Yen in open market	Closes contract for equal loss	Closes contract for gain	Loses equal amount by paying more for Yen in open market

Figure 1.6

Was the Car Dealer Speculating in the Futures Markets?

Now you can see why the financial press is often so hard on futures markets. It is often because they do not understand *why* someone would use them in the first place. With our car dealer example, the dealer was locked into a known expense of $981,250 three months into the future. That's it. Locking in an expense makes perfectly good business sense — especially if the dealer already has the cars sold!

However, in the first scenario where we assumed the yen fell, the dealer realized a "loss" of $1,250. You should now understand why. The dealer entered into a long hedge to guard against *rising* yen prices. If the yen falls, the dealer will lose money on that long asset, just as anyone would who buys high and sells low. What the press fails to see (or conveniently leaves out) is that the car dealer's loss in the long hedge was exactly offset by his ability to buy yen cheaper in the spot market. So was our car dealer speculating in the market? Is this a reckless gambling loss in the futures market? Hopefully you now understand that it isn't, but it certainly could be misconstrued as such if the whole story is not understood.

Futures Price Will Converge to Spot Price

We previously stated that the futures price at expiration would converge to the spot price since the futures price is essentially the spot price near expiration. Now it's time to find out why the two prices are forced to converge. If the futures contract is not trading for (or very close to) the spot price, then arbitrage is possible.

For example, if yen were trading for 7850 in the spot market near expiration in March but the futures contract was trading for 7860, arbitrageurs would buy the currency in the spot market for 7850 and immediately sell the futures contract for 7860 for a guaranteed profit. By selling the futures contract, the arbitrageur must make delivery at 7860 but is assured of doing so, since he already purchased the currency in the spot market at 7850. This activity puts buying pressure on the spot market and selling pressure on the futures price and will eventually bring the two prices together.

Likewise, if yen were trading for 7850 in the spot market but the futures contract was trading for 7840, an arbitrageur would buy the futures contract and sell short the currency in the open market for a guaranteed profit. By purchasing the futures contract, the arbitrageur is accepting the obligation to buy yen at expiration. That's okay since he must do this at some time anyway to cover the short position at 7850. The arbitrageur has guaranteed a "sell high, buy low" trade. This activity puts buying pressure on the futures contract and selling pressure on the spot market and eventually brings the two prices together.

The only way to prevent arbitrage then is for the futures contract price to converge to the spot price at expiration. After all, this is the concept of a futures contract — to determine the spot price in the future. If that future point (expiration) has arrived, obviously the spot price is the same as futures price. Figure 1.7 demonstrates how the individual futures and spot markets are allowed to fluctuate somewhat independently but must meet at expiration:

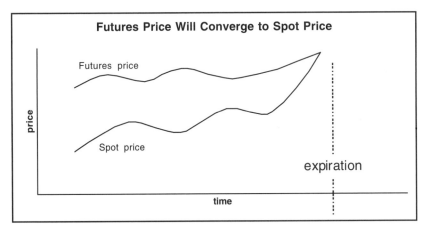

Figure 1.7

With our car dealer example, we said that if the yen spot price fell to 7840 at expiration, the dealer could sell his contract for that amount. Because he entered the contract at 7850, this created a loss of (7850-7840) * 125,000,000 = $1,250. It is because of arbitrage that we know the futures price will converge to the spot price, which ensures our dealer can close out the contract for 7840.

You should now have a better understanding of futures contracts and why they work. The car dealer was able to lock in his purchase price of yen through a standardized contract just as my friend was able to lock in a purchase price of my camera through an informal contract. What made both examples work is that the future transaction price was determined and agreed upon today. The car dealer was using futures contracts in a conservative way and simply locking in a buying price of his upcoming inventory. The seller of the contract may or may not have been conservative. It's possible the seller is a bank that will be selling yen to customers — including the car dealer — in three months. It's also possible that the seller is a speculator and is just betting on a hunch that the yen will fall. It doesn't matter to the car dealer who that person is or why he is short the contract. The fact that he had someone willing to take the short side is all that matters, as the dealer is now able to spread the risk of rising yen prices.

Hopefully you now have an open mind about futures contracts and can continue reading to see how you can benefit from their use in the stock market.

Questions

1) Which of the following is a definition of a futures contract?

   a) Futures contracts give buyers and sellers the right to trade in the future at a price agreed upon today.
   b) Futures contracts allow buyers and sellers to trade in the future at prices agreed upon today.
   c) Futures contracts allow buyers and sellers to trade in the future if the buyer decides to purchase.

2) For the following list of businesses, state whether you'd expect them to be buyers or sellers of futures contracts:

   a) Farmers (buyer/seller)
   b) Kellogg cereal (buyer/seller)
   c) Coca Cola (buyer/seller)
   d) Gold mining company (buyer/seller)
   e) Cotton manufacturer (buyer/seller)
   f) Ralph Lauren (buyer/seller)
   g) Georgia Pacific, which grows trees for lumber (buyer/seller)

3) Futures contracts are the same as options.

   a) True
   b) False

4) Futures contracts were created to allow traders to:

   a) trade at the most favorable prices in the future
   b) legally gamble
   c) hedge price risk

5) If you buy a futures contract, you must buy the underlying asset at expiration of the contract, assuming you do not enter an offsetting position.

   a) True
   b) False

For Questions 6 - 9, assume the following:

A farmer anticipates raising 80,000 pounds of hogs in the next three months for sale. The CME trades lean hog futures contracts worth 40,000 pounds each.

6) If the farmer wishes to hedge price risk, would he be a buyer or seller of the three-month futures contract?

    a) Buyer
    b) Seller

7) How many contracts would the farmer need to enter?
    a) One
    b) Two
    c) One-half
    d) Four

8) If the farmer enters the contract, what type of risk is he exposed to with the futures contract?

    a) Falling prices
    b) Rising prices
    c) Both rising and falling prices

9) If the farmer wishes to get out of the contract, he would:

    a) enter an order to buy the same contract
    b) enter an order to sell the same contract
    c) not be able to get out of a futures contract

10) What's the difference between a forward contract and a futures contract?
    a) There is no difference.
    b) Forwards trade on an exchange while futures do not.
    c) Futures trade on an exchange while forwards do not.

11) A person who is at risk of rising prices would enter a (long/short) futures contract while a person who is at risk of falling prices would enter a (long/short) futures contract.

12) Speculators aid in the functioning of futures markets by:

    a) reducing bid-ask spreads
    b) adding liquidity
    c) promoting price discovery
    d) all of the above

Answers

1) Which of the following is a definition of a futures contract?

    b) Futures contracts allow buyers and sellers to trade in the future at prices agreed upon today

This is just the basic definition stated at the beginning. Answer A is not correct because it says the traders have the right to trade and that is an option. Answer C is also not correct for similar reasons as neither the buyer nor seller get to choose if they will go through with the deal. The only way to get out of a futures contract is with an offsetting position.

2) For the following list of businesses, state whether you'd expect them to be buyers or sellers of futures contracts:

    a) Farmers (seller)

Farmers grow wheat and other agricultural products to sell. If they want to sell these commodities, they would sell wheat futures (and other commodities) to lock in profits.

    b) Kellogg cereal (buyer)

Kellogg buys wheat and other agricultural products to make cereal. They would be buyers of wheat futures (and other grains) to lock in their costs.

    c) Coca Cola (buyer)

Coca Cola uses sugar and corn syrup to make their products. They can hedge price risk by being buyers of these futures contracts.

    d) Gold mining company (seller)

Gold mining companies want to sell gold. They will be sellers of gold futures contracts.

e) Cotton manufacturer (seller)

Cotton manufacturers make cotton for sale. They would be sellers of cotton futures contracts.

f) Ralph Lauren (buyer)

Ralph Lauren buys cotton to make clothes. They would be buyers of cotton futures contracts.

g) Georgia Pacific (seller)

Georgia Pacific grows trees for sale as lumber. They would be sellers of lumber futures.

3) Futures contracts are the same thing as options.

b) False

4) Futures contracts were created to allow traders to:

c) hedge price risk

5) If you buy a futures contract, you must buy the underlying asset at expiration of the contract, assuming you do not enter an offsetting position.

a) True

6) If the farmer wishes to hedge price risk, would he be a buyer or seller of the three-month futures contract?

b) Seller

The farmer has the hogs for sale. Therefore he would be a seller of futures.

7) How many contracts would the farmer need to enter?

b) Two

Each contract controls 40,000 pounds, and he has 80,000 pounds for sale.

8) If the farmer enters the contract, what type of risk is he exposed to with the futures contract?

b) Rising prices

9) If the farmer wishes to get out of the contract, he would:

a) enter an order to buy the same contracts

10) What's the difference between a forward contract and a futures contract?

c) Futures trade on an exchange while forwards do not.

11) A person who is at risk of rising prices rise would enter a *long* futures contract while a person who is at risk of falling prices would enter a *short* futures contract.

12) Speculators aid in the functioning of futures markets by:

d) all of the above

Appendix: Short Selling Basics

You will certainly hear many people talking about "short selling" or "going short" certain stocks as you continue investing. Some people think that short selling isn't necessary and only creates a gambling arena for speculators. Despite the believability of this argument at first glance, speculators actually provide a very important economic function. Without speculators and short sales, the markets would not run as efficiently. If you were only allowed to buy stocks, there would be a tendency for prices to over-inflate, making the markets riskier for those who wish to buy. By allowing short sales, speculators can "cast their vote" on the valuation of a company. If they think it is overvalued, they have a strong incentive to short the stock as they can make a lot of money if they are correct. Without short sales, there is no way for the market to quickly correct for overvalued stocks.

Although short selling can get complicated from a margins perspective, the basics are very easy to understand.

In trader's lingo, you are long a stock if you own it. If you buy 100 shares of IBM, you are long IBM. Of course, the way you make money on a long position is to sell the stock for a higher price than you paid — you want to buy low and sell high. Any position that makes money from a rise in the stock is called a *bullish* position, which is named after the way a bull attacks; it places its horns low and then raises them high. Long stock positions are the most basic investment positions and the ones with which most people are familiar.

However, there are ways to make money during *bear* markets too — when stocks fall from high to low, which is the named after the way a bear attacks with its claws. If you think a stock is going to fall, you can simply call your broker and say you want to sell it short. If you have a short stock position, you borrow shares from your brokerage firm with the promise to return the shares at a later date, which, for the most part, is entirely up to you to decide.

While short selling is usually considered speculative and left for the more sophisticated investors, it does provide two important economic functions — price efficiency and liquidity. Without the ability or incentive to go short, prices could become inflated and take much longer to correct. Also, shorting allows for more sellers, which is good for the conservative buyer as it lowers the stock price.

Shorting stock is similar to buying, just in the opposite order. Rather than buying low and selling high, you are attempting to sell high and buy low. If you have a long position, your broker will debit your account for the cost at the time of purchase and then credit your account the amount when you sell those shares. Short positions occur in the opposite order. First, your broker will credit your account for the sale and then debit your account for the purchase price when you close out the short position. Hopefully you will pay a lower price when you close it out and make a profit from the fall in the stock.

There are some restrictions before you can sell short, though. First, you must have a margin account, which allows you to borrow shares from your broker. In most cases, you just need to fill out a margin agreement form with your broker to get a margin account. Second, the stock must be marginable. If these conditions are met, your broker can get you into a short position with the same speed as a long position. It's not nearly as complicated as it may seem.

There is one more restriction you need to understand. In order for the short sale to execute, it must be done on an uptick. This is nothing you need to be concerned with, as the exchanges will monitor it for you. Just understand that it is possible to not get filled on a short sale (although unlikely) even with a market order.

Example:
Say you are bearish on ABC stock and want to sell it short. Let's run through a trade and see how it works.

With short sales, you must post a minimum of 50% (called the Reg T, or Regulation T amount), which is the same if you buy stocks on margin.

Assume ABC is currently $50; you think it will fall and would like to short 100 shares. The total value of this position is $50 * 100 = $5,000 so you need to post 50% of that, or $2,500, with your broker.

The accounting will look like this:

$$Credit = \$7,500$$
$$-MVS = \$5,000$$
$$=Equity = \$2,500$$

Notice that your equity is $2,500 and when divided by the market value short (MVS) of $5,000 gives you 50% equity, which is the Reg T amount.

Let's assume the stock falls to $40 per share. With the stock at $40, the market value short is now $4,000 and your account looks like this:

$$Credit = \$7,500$$
$$-MVS = \$4,000$$
$$=Equity = \$3,500$$

Notice that the credit balance does not change; it is simply cash sitting in the account. The market value short (MVS) will change, which will change your equity. If the MVS falls, your equity will rise and vice versa, hence a bearish position.

In this example, the stock fell 20% from $50 to $40, giving the investor a 40% increase in equity from $2,500 to $3,500. The reason the investor doubled the move of the stock is because he only posted 50% of the requirement which creates 2:1 leverage.

Because your equity moves in the opposite direction of the stock, short positions are one of the most dangerous as there is no theoretical upper bound on a stock price. For example, if you buy a stock for $50, the most you can lose is $50 if the company goes bankrupt and the stock is trading for zero. However, if you short a stock at $50, there is no upper bound and the stock price can theoretically keep climbing higher and higher. If it climbs quickly, you can be left with negative equity, which means you owe your broker money just to get your account back to a zero balance.

For instance, if ABC in the previous example jumped to $80 the next day on a buyout rumor, your account would look like this:

$$Credit = \$7,000$$
$$-MVS = \$8,000$$
$$=Equity = -\$500$$

Your account is now in negative equity. In other words, you sold stock for $5,000 but now must cover it at $8,000 for a $3,000 loss. Because $2,500 of that loss was your initial equity, you still owe your broker $500, which leaves your account with a zero balance.

Because of the risk of negative equity, brokerage firms have minimum equity requirements to try to prevent you from slipping too far into debt. Most firms require that your equity be at least 35% of the market value short. Note that this is different from the initial Reg T amount, which is always 50%. After the short sale, your account equity is allowed to fluctuate down to about 35% before your broker will require you to bring in more money or else close the position for you.

These are the basics of selling short. As always, you should contact your broker with specific questions regarding their house rules and minimum equity requirements. Short selling is not for everyone as it entails significant risks. But if you balance your risks and rewards and use stop orders or other disciplined approaches for closing out the positions, you may find short positions to be an invaluable strategy.

Chapter 2
The Rewards and Risks
of Futures Contracts

In Chapter 1, we showed you the basics of futures contracts, so you should have a pretty good idea of how they work as well as some basic understanding of the associated advantages and disadvantages. Now it's time to dive deeper into these assets and find out more about the hidden rewards — and risks — associated with futures contracts.

The Rewards:

- Lower margin requirements
- More cash-efficient way to trade
- Greater leverage without interest expense
- Highly liquid
- 24-hour trading
- Global diversification
- No uptick rule to go short
- Long and short positions created with equal ease
- Futures force you to make a decision
- Futures contracts create lower prices

Lower Margin Requirements

If you buy stocks on margin, you can pay for half the amount (subject to a $2,000 minimum) and borrow the other half from your broker. For example, if you buy $10,000 worth of stock, you are only required to pay for half of it (assuming the stock is marginable and you have a margin account). If you choose to do this, you must put down $5,000 of your own money.

Single-stock futures will have a much smaller initial margin requirement, also known as a *performance bond*. The current pro- posed level for futures is 20%. If you buy $10,000 worth of a stock through the futures markets, you would only be required to post $2,000. Some firms even pay interest on these deposits and many will accept bonds at about 90% of face value or stocks at about 50% of face value in lieu of a cash deposit. This will be especially useful since most stock brokerage firms will also trade futures and you can use the stocks or bonds in your portfolio as collateral.

There is another inherent benefit with this lower requirement. It allows for a greater degree of diversification because less capital is required to control the same number of shares. For example, if you have $40,000 to invest, you may only be able to buy a small group of the stocks you'd like to own. Because of the low requirements on futures, you could purchase far more companies thus providing a greater degree of diversification.

More Cash-Efficient Way to Trade

Futures are a trader's dream because of the daily process of marking to market. You'll learn more about marking to market later. For now, just understand that gains will be credited and losses will be debited daily on your account.

To understand why futures are more cash-efficient, let's assume you bought 100 shares of stock at $50 and it is now trading for $60. You have an *unrealized* gain of $1,000 — you have a "paper profit." That unrealized $1,000 could be working for you in other places, even if it's just sitting in the money market earning interest. But you can't get to it without exiting the position. In order to realize that $1,000 and put it in your pocket, you must sell the stock. If you do, you now may miss out on a bigger upward move.

Let's assume, instead, that you had bought the futures contract at $50 and the futures contract is now $60. Because of the daily *mark to market*, your account balance has $1,000 cash sitting in it earning interest. You want to use it to buy more contracts? How about some options? Or maybe you need it for a down payment on a car? Regardless of your needs, the cash is there and you can access it without exiting the position. There is no other financial asset that allows you immediate access to gains without closing the position first.

Greater Leverage Without Interest Expense

We explained in Chapter 1 how futures contracts provide for tremendous leverage. With the proposed 20% initial margin for single-stock futures, that creates 5:1 leverage. With stocks, you could elect to pay for half of the position and borrow the other half from your broker, thus creating 2:1 leverage.

However, if you borrow money from your brokerage firm to buy stocks, you must pay margin interest, which is normally just higher than the broker call rate (also known as the *call money rate*), which can be found daily in *The Wall Street Journal*. The broker call rate is usually lower than most short-term interest rates, including the prime rate or even T-bill rates, due to the fact that brokerages are securing the loans with collateral (stocks). The point is that you get less leverage with stocks and must pay interest to do so! Margin interest can turn out to be a huge expense for stock traders and is one of the main factors that make it so difficult for them to turn a profit over time. The stock may go up and down or even sit flat, but that margin interest keeps accruing on a daily basis.

Remember, buying a futures contract is not the same as buying the underlying asset today. It is a contractual obligation to buy that asset in the future. Therefore, the futures trader is not borrowing money so there is no interest due on a loan.

We can show this in the following example. Assume one person buys 300 shares of stock at $50 and another buys three futures contracts on the same stock. We'll assume both positions are closed at the end of three months with the stock at $58 and that broker call rates are 5% per year. Figure 2.1 compares these two traders:

	300 shares = $15,000	Three futures contracts = $15,000
Initial deposit	$7,500	$3,000
Gain on closing trade	$9,900	$2,400
Gross profit	$2,400	$2,400
Margin interest	93.75	$0
Net profit	$2,306.25	$2,400
Percent gain	30.75%	80%

Figure 2.1

The trader who buys stock must deposit half the amount, or $7,500, and will pay interest on the $7,500 balance he is borrowing. The futures trader, on the other hand, only deposits 20%, or $3,000.

At expiration, with the stock at $58, the stock trader can sell 300 shares at $58 for a total of $17,400 but must repay the $7,500 loan for a gain of $9,900. After subtracting the $7,500 initial deposit, that leaves a profit of $2,400 or a net profit of $2,306.25 after margin interest.[3] Because he initially deposited $7,500, his percentage return is $2,306.25 / $7,500 = 30.75%. We can also show this with some quicker math. The stock rose from $50 to $58, which is a 16% increase. The 50% deposit results in 2:1 leverage for a total return of 32%. However, he must repay 5% * 1/4 year = 1.25% interest for a total gain of 32% - 1.25% = 30.75%.

The futures trader, however, only posts 20% of $15,000, or $3,000. At expiration, the stock is up 8 points for a gain of 8 * 300 = $2,400, which is an 80% return on investment. Notice how the futures trader keeps the full $2,400 since there is no margin interest charge.

Whether you buy stock or an equivalent futures contract, your profits and losses will be exactly the same in terms of total dollars. Both traders in Figure 2.1 made $2,400 gross profit. But due to the lower margin requirement of futures and no margin interest charge, your *percentage returns* will be much greater for futures over stocks.

Highly Liquid

Futures contracts are often highly liquid, which means there are a lot of buyers and sellers at any given time. This is a good quality as it makes the bid-ask spreads narrow and makes it easy to enter or exit a position quickly. We'll talk more about bid-ask spreads and what they mean in Chapter 5. It's one thing to talk about great benefits and strategies associated with futures contracts, but if you can't execute them they're nearly useless. The highly liquid nature of futures contracts ensures that strategies of going long, short, changing

---

[3] The trader borrows $7,500 for three months so he owes $7,500 * 5% * 3/12 months = $93.75 interest.

directional bias, and hedging can all be carried out quickly and efficiently.

24-Hour Trading

The U.S. stock market normally operates between 9:30 a.m. and 4:00 p.m. Eastern Time. This creates a huge problem if some news event occurs and you wish to enter a position or hedge an existing one — you can't do it until the market opens. Futures, however, trade 'round-the-clock through automated systems such as GLOBEX, which is a proprietary computerized trading platform at the CME. Now you can access the markets any time from anywhere in the world. Aside from this benefit, there are other benefits that filter down to the stock market. Because it's easier for investors to access the markets, all information will be disseminated into the stock market quicker, thus creating narrower spreads and lower volatility.

Global Diversification

It can be shown that diversification is the key to minimizing the risk of any stock portfolio for a given level of risk. While the mathematics are beyond the scope of this book, just understand that the ability to access foreign markets with ease is a great advantage to investors. Until now, most who sought global diversification used mutual funds or stocks of companies with global exposure. Mutual funds, however, usually offer a specific country and are rather limited in the selections. Using U.S. stocks as a proxy for global exposure obviously has very limited impact, if any, on your overall portfolio.

Futures though, give you access to many different types of diversification quickly. You want exposure to the Canadian dollar, Euro, British pound, Deutsche mark, or Japanese yen? Or how about something more exotic such as the Australian dollar, South African Rand, Russian ruble, New Zealand dollar, or Swiss franc? It can now be done quickly and easily with futures. You can even get "baskets" of stocks with index futures in Japan, Germany, Taiwan, Italy, and many other countries around the world. In one transaction, you now have immediate and focused exposure to your areas of need.

Maybe there is there an oil crisis. Now you can capitalize by purchasing oil futures. Better yet, buy oil futures and sell airline futures. Futures provide a gateway to capitalize when world events impact the financial markets. You cannot get international exposure more efficiently than with futures contracts.

No Uptick Rule to Go Short

We said in Chapter 1 that traders could make money from a downturn in stock price by going short. However, there are several stipulations:

- The stock must be marginable
- Your broker must be able to locate the shares to short
- You are subject to hefty margin requirements
- The short sale must be done on an uptick, which means you may receive an unfavorable price

The one stipulation that hangs most short sellers is the uptick rule. What is an uptick? Very simply, any change in the price of a security is known as a *tick*. For instance, if a stock is trading at $100 with the next trade being $100.10, that's an uptick — the change in price was up. Likewise, if the next trade were back down to $100, that trade would be a downtick.

What happens if there's no change in price? Let's say the next trade was from $100 to $100.25 (uptick) and then the following trade was also at $100.25. This last trade is said to take place on a zero-plus tick. That means there was no change between it and the previous trade or trades, but if we look back to the last time a change occurred ($100), it would be a plus tick. In fact, if you look at the system you use to get quotes, you will likely see a + or - sign in front of the last trades, which designates whether that stock or index is trading on an uptick or downtick (some systems will show the trades in green for uptick or red for downtick, or even up and down arrows). The reason the exchanges track ticks is that any short sale must be done on an uptick or zero-plus tick.

This can create problems for the short seller. If you see an opportunity and wish to go short, you must wait for an uptick (or zero plus tick) before the trade can be executed, even if you enter a market order. For example, say the stock is trading for $100, negative news hits, and you enter an order to sell short 300 shares at market. Because of the news, the stock is in a freefall and is trading on downticks, with the tape showing the following trades:

100, -99.75, -99.50, -99, -98.50, -98, -97.75,
-97.25, -96.50, -96, -95.75, +95.80

Your trade would be filled on the uptick at $95.80 even though you entered the order when it was trading at $100. The exchanges imposed this rule after the Crash of '87 to prevent traders from short-selling stocks that are in a freefall thus putting more downward pressure on them and nearly guaranteeing an unfair profit. Another problem this rule creates for traders is that by the time upticks start to show, that may be close to the equilibrium point of the stock's price and it ends up stabilizing at the price where you sold. It can be frustrating when your judgment leads you in the right direction but a market restriction keeps you from profiting. This is not to say that the uptick rule shouldn't be in place; it just creates problems for those wanting to short stocks.

In fact, it is for this reason that the stock market has a "sell short" order that is separate from a "sell" order. There is a need to separate the two orders since a sell short order is bound by the uptick rule. With futures you either buy or sell. If you wish to be short a futures contract, you enter an order to sell and you're short. It's that simple.

Long and Short Positions Created with Equal Ease

This may sound like a rewording of the previous benefit. However, we're talking about a little different aspect here in the sense of the margin requirements. If you short a $100 stock, you must put up half that amount (Reg T requirement) and post $50 cash or margin cash. Let's say you want to short 1,000 shares at $50. You must put up $25,000 of your own money in order to do so. In addition, individual firms may have stricter requirements, especially if the stock is volatile, and they may require more money up front.

With futures contracts, people are agreeing to buy and sell at some point in the future. Both parties post (pay) the same requirements and then are marked to market daily. If you sell a futures contract valued at $50,000, you will only be required to post 20%, which makes it much cheaper to establish short positions. Whether you are long or short a futures contract does not matter from a margin standpoint, but it can make a big difference with stocks!

Futures Force Disciplined Trading

Because of the daily mark to market process with futures, they force you to make a decision rather than taking a passive route. For example, you may have bought a stock that trends down slightly, day after day. Eventually, you're in a larger-than-expected loss and it becomes that much more difficult to sell it for a loss. Many times you will end up hanging on to it only to watch it slip further. Futures contracts, however, will force you to take a closer look at the position and your decision to buy (sell) it. If you keep sending money to your broker for daily mark to market, or for variation margin, it will cause you to make an active decision to continue holding it. If you hold fully paid-for stock, however, it's much easier to ignore the downturn and end up with much larger losses. Futures contracts force a more disciplined trading style.

Futures Contracts Create Lower Prices

Besides hedging risks for individuals or corporations, futures contracts provide another important economic benefit for all of us — they create lower prices of the underlying assets. For example, farmers are more willing to grow wheat if they know they can lock in a sales price today. The wheat takes time to grow, but the risk of a lower sales price is removed through the futures markets. With reduced risk, farmers are willing to provide more wheat so the supply rises and wheat prices fall, which is better for everyone who is a buyer of wheat.

On the other side of the farmer's trade, a cereal manufacturer may wish to buy wheat for its next operating quarter. The rising price uncertainty it would usually face is a deterrent to manufacturing cereal. Faced with this risk, cereal companies tend to produce less cereal. Why would a cereal company want to take orders for millions of boxes of cereal from grocery stores if it's not sure it can provide them at a profit? In fact, if wheat costs rise significantly, the company could end up with huge losses or even bankruptcy. The futures markets remove the risk of rising prices so cereal companies can provide a larger supply — and lower prices — of cereal.

The Risks:

- You could lose more than your initial investment
- Leverage/emotional risks
- Limits moves in the underlying
- Basis risk

As with any financial asset, the great rewards and benefits of any product do not come without some sort of risk. While this is not an exhaustive list, we will attempt to address most of the risks associated with futures trading.

You Could Lose More Than Your Initial Investment

As we've stated before, futures are not options and you can lose more than your initial margin deposit. Remember, the initial deposit is a "good faith" deposit, and you will either deliver or take delivery of the underlying asset at the predetermined price, assuming you do not enter an offsetting contract. If you buy the contract and the futures price falls significantly, you will be required to deposit more money. Theoretically, if the price move is large enough, you could end up with negative equity, which means you must send your broker a check just to get your account balance back to zero. Normally this is not a concern because of the daily price limits allowed on most commodities. However, with single-stock futures, there are no daily price limits, so your account values could swing significantly.

Of course, the way to manage this risk is to monitor your positions closely and to not let losses run against you too long. In fact, many futures firms offer managed accounts where the broker will trade your account for you, which can certainly be an advantage if the broker has the same trading ideals as you.

Leverage/Emotional Risks

We explained earlier that leverage is an asset and now we're showing that it is also a risk. This is consistent with our earlier comment that leverage is a double-edged sword — it can work for and against you.

While the physical leverage qualities are a risk in itself, what's probably more of a risk is the emotional risk that is tied with it. Can you stand to see hundreds or thousands of dollars vaporized from your account in a potentially short time? Will you have the discipline to exit the position? Or maybe the better move is to sit tight, do nothing, and maintain your convictions. If so, will you be able to do that? It's one thing to *say* that you can, but an entirely different one when you're dealing with real money. It is this highly emotional state that can cause you to make the wrong decision. Understand that emotional risk exists, even among professionals; and know your limits.

Limit Moves in the Underlying

Most commodity contracts have daily price limits — upper and lower bounds — that cannot be exceeded during the day. If a boundary is broken to the upside, that commodity is said to be *locked limit up* or just *limit up* for the day. Similarly, if it is to the downside it is limit down. Assume you are short a contract and wish to buy it back. However, the underlying commodity is limit up and trades can only occur inside this range. While trades can occur inside this range, do you think anyone is going to sell to you if they are reasonably sure it will be higher tomorrow? If not, commodities can remain limit up for extended periods of time and never give you the chance to exit. After all, if the price is 100 today and, after new information, the market values the commodity at 120, the trading should theoretically not take place until the price is 120, even if it takes many limit up days to get there. Single-stock futures will not have daily price limits, which can be good and bad. While you will never be locked out of a trade, you will also never have limited moves to reduce losses. In Chapter 6 we'll show you how to protect yourself in case this happens to you while trading a commodity with price limits.

Basis Risk

We explained in Chapter 1 that the futures price converges to the spot price. The difference between the futures price and spot price is called the spread or basis.[4] That difference will shrink as expiration nears; however, the rate at which the two prices converge *prior to expiration* can vary, and the uncertainty associated with it is called basis risk.

Basis risk is often considered a risk for hedgers, but is a significant risk for speculators as well. For example, say the S&P 500 index is at 1,000 and you are long a three-month S&P futures contract at 1010. At this point, the spread, or basis, is 10 — the futures price minus the spot price. We know at expiration the basis will be zero since the futures price and spot price must be the same. But let's say you get out of the contract early with the spot index at 1015. You should be up five points from your purchase price of 1010. However, because futures and spot markets are different, they are subject to their own sets of supply and demand. You may go to close the contract and find it is trading for 1012. If so, your expected five-point profit has been reduced to two points — that's basis risk.

Basis risk is a real problem for hedgers. Imagine the car dealer in Chapter 1 who bought futures on the Japanese yen to lock in a purchase price for the cars. If his payment is due *before* the contract expires, those futures contracts may not provide a full hedge and he could still end up with a loss. This problem is compounded by the fact that futures contracts will rarely expire on the exact day you need them to, which leaves you exposed to basis risk. Let's take a look at some specific examples of basis risk.

---

[4] For commodities, the basis is usually defined as the spot price minus the futures price. However, it is conventional for financial assets to define the basis as futures price minus spot price. Because we are primarily dealing with financial assets in this book, we will use this convention.

Example 1: Basis Risk of a Short Hedge

In Chapter 1, we assumed a Lexus dealer had to purchase 125,000,000 Japanese yen in three months. Let's continue with that example and understand that the Japanese manufacturer, Lexus, will be *receiving* that many yen in three months. It will also likely wish to hedge that cash inflow. Its concern is that the value of the yen may fall between now and then, so hopefully you know that Lexus will need a short hedge — it must sell the Japanese yen contract.

In our original example, we assumed the car dealer would take delivery in three months and also buy a matching three-month contract. But let's add a twist this time. Let's say the delivery will be made in two months and that Lexus will take delivery of Japanese yen at that time but sell a three-month contract. Why would they sell a three-month contract? Because a two-month contract may not exist. Remember, futures are standardized contracts as to size and time, so you don't always get the perfect choice.

Lexus will wish to protect the entire 125,000,000 yen it will receive, so it'll need to sell 10 contracts, which we'll assume are sold for 7850. This means it is expecting to receive 125,000,000 yen from the car dealer in two months at a price of $.007850, a value of $981,250. The important point to understand about basis risk is this: If the value of the yen is down in two months, the dealer is expecting to profit from the gain in the futures contract to offset that loss.

Two months pass and the yen is, in fact, down and trading for 7800. However, the contract, which has not expired yet, is trading for 7820. Remember, at expiration, the futures price will converge to the spot price. But prior to expiration, the two will not be trading for the same value. Lexus takes delivery of the 125,000,000 yen, which is worth $975,000 rather than the $981,250 it was expecting. However, its short futures contract will be trading for a higher price, so it can offset this loss. The gain on the futures contract is 7850 - 7820 = 0.0030. Therefore, Lexus will make 0.000030 * 125,000,000 = $3,750 from the sale of the contract for a total cash inflow of $975,000 + $3,750 = $978,750, which is a $2,500 shortfall from the $981,250 they were expecting.

This is basis risk from a short hedge. It occurred because the contract had not expired at the time the hedger (Lexus) needed to get out of the contract. Had Lexus been able to sell a two-month contract, the futures price would have converged to the spot price and would have left it with no shortfall.

Example 2: Basis Risk of a Long Hedge

We can use the same example to show basis risk of a long hedge. All we have to do is look at it in terms of the hedger on the other side — the long futures contract. Let's assume the U.S. Lexus dealer buys 10 three-month contracts at 7850 but must take delivery of the cars in two months. The car dealer realizes he is going to pay 125,000,000 * .007850 = $981,250 in two months and wishes to hedge any price increases in the yen by purchasing the yen contract. This long hedge will rise in value if the yen should rise, which will offset his costs.

At the time of delivery, the yen is trading for 7860 but the futures contract is only trading for 7857. The dealer, expecting to pay $981,250 must now pay 125,000,000 * .007860 = $982,500. Because the yen is higher, he can sell his 10 futures contracts at a profit to offset his cost. However, he will only receive a profit of (.007857 - .007850) = $875. His costs were $1,250 higher but he only receives $875 of this back from his futures contract — that's basis risk of a long hedge.

You may be thinking, "Why doesn't the car dealer use his futures contract and just purchase the yen for 7850?" Remember, futures are not options. The futures contract expires in one more month, and in that contract, that's the agreed upon time to buy and sell the yen — not today. The dealer can therefore only use it as a hedge but, as we just showed, those hedges do not always work perfectly. Of course, it's possible that the dealer may wish to purchase an extra contract to make up for any losses through basis risk. That's certainly okay to do and happens quite frequently in practice. However, it does not come for free as the dealer must post more money for the initial margin requirement, which may or may not be advantageous from a business standpoint.

We can show the effects of basis risk mathematically. Assume a futures contract price today is F_1 and F_2 when it is closed. Likewise, the price of the underlying stock is S_1 today and S_2 at the time the futures contract is closed. From our previous definition, we know that basis is the difference between the futures price and spot price so the basis today, B_1, is:

$$B_1 = F_1 - S_1$$

Similarly, the basis in the future is:

$$B_2 = F_2 - S_2$$

Consider our U.S. car dealer who purchased a three-month contract to hedge the purchase price of yen two months in the future.

At the time the contract was purchased, the spot price was S_1 and the futures were purchased for F_1. When the contract was closed, the car dealer purchased yen in the open market at a higher price, S_2, and received F_2 from the sale of the contract. His total gain on the futures contract is therefore $(F_2 - F_1)$ and he spends S_2 for yen in the spot market. The car dealer's total cash flows are then:

$$(F_2 - F_1) - S_2$$

This can be rearranged as:

$$(F_2 - S_2) - F_1$$

However, $F_2 - S_2 = B_2$ so we can rewrite the car dealer's cash flows when he closes the contract as:

$$B_2 - F_1$$

It is the uncertainty of the future basis that poses the risk for this long hedge used by the car dealer. He receives B_2 and purchases the contract for a price of F_1 for a net gain of $B_2 - F_1$. It is evident that the unknown spread between the futures price and spot price, the basis, is what presents a real risk to futures traders.

We'll show in Chapter 4 how arbitrage will keep the futures and spot prices reasonably close together so basis risk is not without bounds. In fact, the basis is more predictable for financial futures than it is for commodities due to minimal storage costs for financials.

However, if you are trading a large number of contracts (or if the multiplier on the contract is large) and using them to hedge, just be aware that you could still come up short because of basis risk.

The basis, we said, is defined as the difference between the futures price and the spot price, which can be written as:

Basis = F - S

F is the futures price and S is the spot price of the underlying asset. If the futures price rises by a larger amount than the spot price, the basis will increase. This is known as a strengthening of the basis — the spread is getting bigger. Likewise, if the spot price rises faster than the futures price, the basis will shrink, which is known as a weakening of the basis.

While it is possible to come up short due to basis risk, it's also possible it may help you, too. For instance, in the first example where we looked at basis risk of a short hedge we assumed the Japanese firm (Lexus) sold the yen contracts to protect its price at the time of delivery. If the yen falls relative to the dollar, then Lexus will offset their losses with the short futures contracts that will rise in value. But suppose the yen falls; since we are not at expiration, the price of the futures contract falls more than the spot price — a weakening of the basis. If so, Lexus makes more money from the futures hedge than is necessary to offset its losses on the yen. If you are short the futures contract, a weakening basis will help you.[5] Similarly, if you are long a futures contract, then a strengthening basis will help you. It will provide money above what is necessary to offset your losses from any increases in the spot price.

---

[5] This is assuming our definition of the basis, which is futures price minus spot price. If you use the conventional definition, which is spot price minus futures price, you will get the opposite answer — a short futures position will be helped by a strengthening of the basis.

Chapter 3
Single-Stock Futures

Now that you have a basic understanding of futures contracts, you should be able to see their advantages. Hopefully you have a strong interest in finding out more. Until now, most investors have had little to no use for them, since they are ordinarily traded on commodities. But, as stated in Chapter 1, single-stock futures will start trading soon. Once they start trading, there will be no need to learn the futures market by buying and selling pork bellies, cocoa, or benzene. You'll be able to buy and sell contracts on the stocks you know and understand with the same benefits that commodity futures traders have had for years.

Why did it take so long for the idea of single-stock futures to catch on?

The Shad-Johnson Accord

Actually, it didn't take long to catch on. It just took a long time to get the idea's regulation approved due to political control reasons. Stock index futures began trading at the Chicago Mercantile Exchange in 1982, which included the popular S&P 500 index contract (Standard & Poor's 500). It was at this time that single-stock futures and narrow based indices were also being considered, but were stalled over concerns of which regulatory body would control them. Should these contracts be regulated through the Securities and Exchange Commission (SEC), who controls the equity markets or should it be controlled through the Commodities Futures Trading Commission (CFTC), which is the governing body of the futures markets?

The debates became heated and drawn out between SEC Chairman John Shad and CFTC Chairman Phil Johnson until Congress suspended the idea of SSFs futures to prevent holding up the index futures through a bill known as the Shad-Johnson Accord.

Commodities Futures Modernization Act (CFMA)

In December 1999, various Congressional committees pushed for a plan, which would lift the nearly 20-year ban on single-stock futures. The result was the Commodities Futures Modernization Act (CFMA) and was signed into law one year later by President Clinton. The trading of these assets was scheduled for September 2001, but the terrorist attacks on the U.S. delayed their introduction. We can expect to see single-stock futures trading in the U.S. as early as July 15, 2002 and are just waiting for ruling on initial margin and maintenance requirements (explained later in the chapter) as well as taxation rulings from the Internal Revenue Service.

It was critical for the CFMA to be passed, as SSFs were already trading in Europe through contracts known as *Universal Stock Futures*, which started in January 2001 on the London International Financial Futures and Options Exchange (LIFFE). These universal stock futures were quickly gaining popularity — 20 of which were U.S. companies — and there was fear that the European exchanges would control the trading of these viable assets. The U.S. wanted to remain the leader in financial markets and had to pass the CFMA in order to not lose this business to overseas markets.

New Products Form New Exchanges: OneChicago and Nasdaq-Liffe

Brand-new electronic futures exchanges will be created to trade this hybrid stock and futures product. Technically, any exchange can file to trade these products, but presently there are two that will begin trading SSFs immediately: OneChicago and Nasdaq-Liffe Markets (NQLX).

OneChicago is comprised of the three largest exchanges in the world for futures and options — the CME (Chicago Mercantile Exchange), CBOT (Chicago Board of Trade) and CBOE (Chicago Board Options Exchange).

On the Nasdaq-Liffe (pronounced LIFE) exchange, the LIFFE brings a lot of experience to the partnership with its LIFFE

CONNECT™ trading system, which is the world's most advanced electronic derivatives trading platform already capable of handling large order flow, while the Nasdaq will blend its state-of-the-art technologies to make single-stock futures as well as narrow-based indices (collectively called *single futures products*, or SFPs) and provide a highly efficient platform to trade these exciting new products.

The First Wave

Any time a significant change is made in the securities markets, the regulators always manage the change slowly just in case there are any bugs in the system. Typically they move the companies over in blocks of 50, which is what happened when the industry moved to after-hours trading and decimalization. The same process will be used with SSFs, and the first 50 companies expected to begin trading are a mixture between those listed on the New York Stock Exchange (NYSE) or traded on the Nasdaq:

Nasdaq-Liffe Markets Initial Stock Listing (as of February 1, 2002)*

Stock	Symbol	GICS Group	Exchange
Advanced Micro Devices	AMD	Semiconductor Equiptment & Products	NYSE
American International Group	AIG	Insurance	NYSE
Amgen Inc.	AMGN	Biotechnology	Nasdaq
AOL Time Warner	AOL	Media	NYSE
Applied Materials	AMAT	Semiconductor Equipment & Products	Nasdaq
AT&T Corp.	T	Diversified Telecommunications Services	NYSE
Bank of America Corp.	BAC	Diversified Financial	NYSE
Bristol-Myers Squibb	BMY	Pharmaceuticals	NYSE
Brocade Communications System	BRCD	Communications Equipment	Nasdaq
ChevronTexaco	CVX	Oil & Gas	NYSE
Cisco Systems Inc.	CSCO	Communications Equipment	Nasdaq
Citigroup Inc.	C	Diversified Financial	NYSE
Coca Cola Co.	KO	Beverages	NYSE
Dell Computer Corp.	DELL	Computers & Peripherals	Nasdaq
eBay	EBAY	Internet & Catalogue	Nasdaq
EMC Corp/Massachusetts	EMC	Computer - Peripherals	NYSE
Exxon Mobil	XOM	Oil & Gas	NYSE
Ford Motor	F	Automobiles	NYSE
General Electric	GE	Industrial Conglomerate	NYSE
General Motors	GM	Automobiles	NYSE
Genzyme Corp-General Division	GENZ	Biotechnology	Nasdaq
Hewlett-Packard Co.	HPQ	Computers	NYSE

Stock	Symbol	GICS Group	Exchange
Home Depot	HD	Specialty Retail	NYSE
Honeywell International Inc.	HON	Aerospace & Defense	NYSE
International Business Machines Corp.	IBM	Computers & Peripherals	NYSE
Intel Corp.	INTC	Semiconductor Equipment & Products	Nasdaq
Johnson & Johnson	JNJ	Pharmaceuticals	NYSE
JP Morgan Chase & Co.	JPM	Diversified Financial	NYSE
Juniper Networks Inc.	JNPR	Communication Equipment	Nasdaq
Merck	MRK	Pharmaceuticals	NYSE
Merrill Lynch & Co. Inc.	MER	Diversified Financial	NYSE
Micron Technology Inc.	MU	Semiconductor Equipment & Products	NYSE
Microsoft Corp.	MSFT	Software	Nasdaq
Morgan Stanley Dean Witter & Co.	MWD	Diversified Financial	NYSE
Oracle Corp.	ORCL	Software	Nasdaq
PepsiCo Inc.	PEP	Beverages	NYSE
Pfizer Inc.	PFE	Pharmaceuticals	NYSE
Proctor & Gamble	PG	Household Products	NYSE
Qualcomm Inc.	QCOM	Communications Equipment	Nasdaq
SBC Communications Inc.	SBC	Diversified Telecommunications Services	NYSE
Siebel Systems Inc.	SEBL	Software	Nasdaq
Sun Microsystems Inc.	SUNW	Computers & Peripherals	Nasdaq
Texas Instruments Inc.	TXN	Semiconductor Equipment & Products	Nasdaq
Veritas Software Corp.	VRTS	Software	NYSE
Verizon Communications Inc.	VZ	Diversified Telecommunications Services	NYSE
Wal-Mart Stores Inc.	WMT	Multiline Retail	NYSE
Walt Disney Company	DIS	Media	NYSE

* Stocks listed are subject to change

Mechanics of a Single-Stock Futures Trade

The mechanics of buying and selling a futures contract is very similar to stock. If you buy the futures contract, you want the price to move higher. If you short (sell) the futures contract, you want the price to fall. From a profit and loss standpoint, a long futures position looks just like a long stock position, as shown in Figure 3.1:

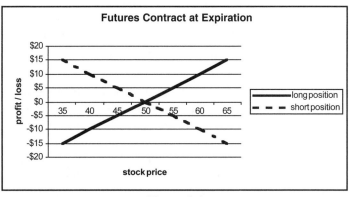

Figure 3.1

Compare this to a long $50 call option in Figure 3.2 below. We can see that call options provide an *asymmetrical payoff* meaning that profit and losses do not occur in a straight line over all stock prices. We said in Chapter 1 that long futures contracts behave like long deep-in-the-money call options. You can see from Figure 3.2 that this would be true for all stock prices above $50 at expiration, as that is the portion of the call option payoff represented by a straight line. Whether the stock rises or falls in this range, the long call owner will gain or lose point for point just as a long futures holder would. However, if the stock falls below $50, the call option owner limits the losses. While limited losses are a big advantage of options, keep in mind there is no time premium paid, other than the cost of carry, for the futures position. The value of the long futures contract will not decay from the passage of time as a long call option would.

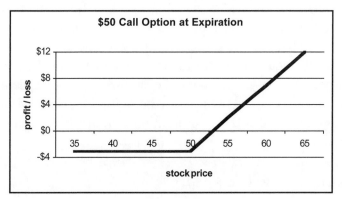

Figure 3.2

We can show how a long futures contract behaves like a long stock position with an example. Assume it is January and Microsoft is trading for $60. You think it will rise substantially over the next six months, and you wish to buy 500 shares of stock. As an alternative, you could call your broker and buy a six-month futures contract. Let's assume the futures price is $61.50 — we'll explain why in the next chapter.

If you bought 500 shares of the stock, you could pay for it using one of two methods: First, you could pay the $60 up front and spend $30,000. Second, you could elect to use margin and only pay for 50% of the amount, Reg T, which is $15,000. Of course, if you only pay for half of the trade, you are borrowing the remainder from the brokerage firm and will pay interest on that balance.

With the futures contract, however, you will pay a much smaller percentage, known as *initial margin* (or a *performance bond*), which at the time of this writing is proposed to be 20% for single-stock futures. If you were required to deposit 20%, you could buy five contracts (equivalent to 500 shares) and only pay 500 * $61.50 * 0.20 = $6,150 initial margin. You'd be controlling $30,000 worth of stock for only $6,150 down, as opposed to $15,000 under current stock rules.

This 20% figure is just a guideline for several reasons. First, as with stocks, individual firms are allowed to make stricter requirements, so they could certainly make the requirements higher than those determined by the exchange. Second, as fluctuations in the underlying stock rise and fall, the exchanges can, and do, alter the requirements to keep the margin in line with the current volatility. Third, margin requirements for futures often depend on the objectives of the trader, too. If you are a retail customer making a speculative trade, your requirements will likely be higher than that of a bona fide hedger, such as a large corporation selling futures against anticipated delivery of the underlying asset.

Marking to Market

Notice in the above example that when you "pay $61.50" for this contract, that's just the agreed upon price six months into the future. You do not pay $61.50 now. So why must you pay anything? The reason is that due to the extreme leverage (controlling a lot of shares for only a little money down), losses can quickly mount. To keep the rock-solid credit worthiness of the futures markets, the exchanges credit your account with any gains and debit your account for any losses on a daily basis. This is done at the end of the first day you enter the trade and at the close of each trading day thereafter. This process is known as *marking* to *market* — the account is being *marked* to the *market* price of the underlying asset.

The exchanges usually allow for minor fluctuations and will permit your account to lose some value before requiring you to bring in more money. That level is called maintenance margin and, if reached, you will be required to bring your account back up to initial margin levels. The maintenance margin levels vary but are typically about 20% to 25% below the initial margin levels. It is possible, however, that the initial margin levels and maintenance margin levels will be the same amounts for single-stock futures.

For example, say you entered the five contracts at $61.50 and paid $6,150 initial margin with a $4,920 maintenance margin, which is 20% below the initial $6,150 initial margin. The next day the stock is up, and the futures contract is trading for $62.50. The easiest way to calculate your gains or losses is to take the net change of the futures contract, which is $1 in this example, and multiply it by the number of shares you are controlling: 500 shares *$1 rise in price = $500 credit. Therefore, your account would be credited with $500 cash and the person on the other side of your trade, the short contract, would be debited this amount. Your account is now worth $6,150 + $500 = $6,650.

Whether or not you close out your futures contract doesn't matter — your account will be credited $500 at the end of the trading day. You are free to leave the $500 in the account or withdraw it. Most people leave the cash in, since fluctuations in the stock price may cause you to reach maintenance levels, and credits to your account provide a cushion against this.

Now assume the futures contract closes at $60.50 the following day, down $2. Since the position is down $2 from the previous day's close, your account will be debited 500 * -$2 = $1,000 cash, and the short position will be credited with $1,000 cash. Your account is always marked to market on a daily basis according to the change in closing prices.

Your account was worth $6,650 and is now worth $5,650, so it's still okay — it has not hit the $4,920 maintenance level.

But assume the futures contract closes down another $2 the next day at $58.50. Your account will be debited another 5 contracts * -$2 = $1,000 debit for a total account value of $4,650, which is below the hypothetical maintenance level of $4,920. You will now receive a *maintenance call* from your broker and be required to bring the account back to the initial margin level of $6,150 by depositing $1,500.[6] The deposit you make is called *variation margin*.

Let's assume that Microsoft is trading for $75 near expiration, which is up 25% from $60. Because we know the futures price will converge to the spot price, the futures contract will be trading for $75 as well. Through all of the possible debits and credits that could occur in your account along the way up to the $75 price, your account would now be up +$15 * 500 contracts or $7,500 for a total value of $13,500. You put $6,150 down and can close out the contract, which leaves you with $13,500 in the account for roughly a 120% gain even though the stock only moved 25%.

This magnification in return on investment is known as *leverage*. Had you invested in the stock, your return would equal the move in the stock and you'd have made 25% on your money. But because you were required to only pay for a fraction of the value of the stock, you leveraged your money and made 120% with the futures contract. The leverage, in this example, is purely a reflection of the initial margin amount of 20%, or 1/5 the amount of the stock price. Therefore, the gains will be the reciprocal amount, or five times greater. Notice how 25% * 5 = 125%. The reason the account is

---

[6] It has not yet been determined whether the industry will require investors to bring their equity to the original margin requirement or if that margin requirement will be allowed to float with subsequent futures prices. For our purposes, we will assume you must meet the original margin level, which is a more conservative stance.

up 120% and not 125% is because we paid $61.50 for the futures contract when the stock was trading for $60. The additional $1.50 paid is due to the cost of carry — that's the interest lost by the stockholder who buys stock to make delivery on the futures contract. Because his money is tied up in the stock, he misses out on the interest he could have earned. The futures buyer must pay this missing interest. Again, we'll explain why in the next chapter.

For now, just understand that futures contracts provide roughly five times the return of stocks. If we ignore the cost of carry, then for any given percentage gain in the stock, your return will be exactly five times greater (assuming you're only required to put down 20%) with a futures contract.

Leverage can be your best friend and is the one variable that has been a key factor in many great success stories in the market. However, it can also be your worst nightmare and is the same variable that has destroyed many speculators and even corporations. Nick Leeson destroyed the historic Baring's Bank by recklessly gambling in the futures market in an attempt to support some options positions that had already gone bad. If the leverage is great enough, even well capitalized banks cannot withstand the pressures.

Leverage is a double-edged sword because it works the other direction, too, and magnifies losses in the same aggressive manner. Let's assume that, instead, Microsoft were to end up trading for $50. While there may be many debits and credits to your account along the way to that $50 price, the bottom line is that the stock is now trading for $50. Your account is down $10 * 500 = $5,000 and is worth a total of $1,150. You started with $6,150 and ended up with $1,150 for an 81.3% loss on a 16.6% decrease in the stock. Again, notice how that five-fold leverage factor works to the downside as well. A 16.6% decrease in the stock results in a 16.6% * 5 = 83% decrease in your account value. Once again, the figures do not match up exactly, due to the differences in pricing of the futures contract compared to the stock.

With a 20% initial margin requirement, the futures contracts provide a five-fold multiplier to the gains and losses in the underlying stock. It's sometimes difficult to understand this multiplying effect, but it's always there. Those who do not understand leverage with investments eventually learn the hard way. Make sure you understand just how much leverage you're dealing with before you enter in to a contract; buy or sell the appropriate number of contracts you are comfortable with — especially if you are speculating!

Differences Between Futures and Forwards

Forward agreements, as we said earlier, are independent agreements between two people to buy and sell an asset for a fixed price in the future. In the case of forwards, profits and losses are not realized until that future date. If the previous example were a forward contract at a price of $60, we wouldn't realize our $7,500 gain until expiration. It wouldn't matter how high or low the stock moved in the meantime. The only thing that matters to a forward contract is where it ends up at expiration. This is one of the big dangers of forward contracts, especially if the integrity of the other party is questionable. If the forward contract moves against them substantially, all of the losses are due at expiration and it is possible they may default on the agreement.

Futures contracts, however, realize profits and losses daily through the process of *marking to market. In effect, futures contracts are closed and rewritten at a new price each day.* With futures contracts, price swings would cause intermediate gains or losses. For comparison purposes, let's assume the Microsoft futures contract is purchased for $60 rather than the $61.50 we originally used, which means we would only pay $6,000 initial margin. This will make it easier to compare to the $60 forward contract.

With a $60 futures contract, the end result is that we would be up $7,500 when the stock reached $75 just as with a forward contract. But during the time we hold the futures contract, price changes will make a difference to us. To understand this, let's assume that Microsoft's price moved only three times during the six-month period from $60 down to $58, up to $68, and then up again to $75.

With the stock down $2 at $58, your account would be debited -$2 * 500 = -$1,000, for a total account value of $5,000. This debit to the account *effectively* closes out the original contract to buy at $60 and rewrites the contract to buy for the current price of $58. Buying 500 shares at $58 costs $29,000 coupled with the $1,000 loss to the account equals the original purchase price of $30,000, which is 500 shares at $60.

Next the stock moves up to $68. Your account will now be credited $10 * 500 = $5,000 for a total value of $10,000. Effectively the contract has been closed to buy at $58 and rewritten to buy the shares at $68. Buying 500 shares at $68 costs $34,000, but you've been credited a total of $4,000 so your effective price is still the original $30,000.

Now the stock makes its final move to $75. Again, you'd be credited $7 * 500 = $3,500 for a total account value of $13,500, which is what we calculated using a forward agreement. Figure 3.3 compares the changes in account value for forwards and futures across the various stock prices:

	$60 Forward Account Value	$60 Futures Account Value
Initial Deposit	$6,000	$6,000
Price	**Change in account value**	
$58	No change	-$1,000
$68	No change	+$5,000
$75	No change	+$3,500
Contract expires	+$13,500	+$13,500

Figure 3.3

Please keep in mind this example demonstrates that marking to market is a *mathematical equivalent* of closing the existing contract and rewriting a new one at the spot price on a daily basis. The contracts are not actually closed and rewritten, but they are on a conceptual basis. If you wish to close out a contract, you must enter an order for the offsetting contract.

Marking to Market Is Based on Settlement Prices

Now you should have a better understanding as to why your account is marked to market based on comparisons of closing (settlement) prices rather than comparisons of closing prices to contract prices. That's because marking to market effectively rewrites the contract price by either debiting or crediting your account.

For example, if you bought the 5 Microsoft futures for $60 and they close at $63 the next day, you'd be up $3 * 500 = $1,500. But say they close at $61 down $2 the following day. Many people new to futures incorrectly think they will be credited $1 * 500 = $500 since they are under contract at $60 and the futures closed at $61. The reason that's wrong is because the investor effectively rewrote the contract at $63 when they accepted the $1,500 credit the first day.

If you're still not sure, think about what would happen if the futures closed back at $60 on the second day. Do you think it's fair to say that because there's no change between the closing price and your contract price, your account is left unchanged, yet you get to keep the $1,500 from the first day? If your contract price is $60 and the futures close at $60, your account should be unchanged in total equity. The only way to make that happen is to say your account is down $3 (from settlement prices of $63 to $60). You should be debited $1,500 leaving your account unchanged.

Marking to market allows traders to effectively close out positions and rewrite new contracts on a daily basis without having to do so. It is a procedure that allows gains and losses to mount on a daily basis rather than having to wait until expiration. This is truly an advantage of using standardized contracts by marking them to market on a daily basis. It keeps losses from continuing to mount all the way through expiration and discovers those who are risk of default in the early stages.

Which Contracts Will Be Traded?

Just as with options, futures only provide for a limited number of expiration months at any given time, which is yet another disadvantage

Daily Price Limits   73

of standardized contracts. Regardless, there are usually enough expiration months to satisfy most investors. Remember, the exchange aims to make a profit, and if a lot of people are requesting additional months, they will certainly change the rules and issue new months. So despite the limited number, you probably won't feel restricted.

Single-stock futures contracts will be available with expirations for the first five calendar quarters (March, June, September, December) and in the first two non-quarter calendar months for a total of seven months. For example, if it were now June, contracts would be available for June and July — the current month (also called the spot month) and the following month. In addition, there would be September and December of the same year and March, June, and September of the following year. This method ensures that the first three months will be traded at any given time. So for now, you'll be able to take positions in single-stock futures up to 15 months away; this will likely change as their popularity grows.

Size and Expiration of Contracts

Just like equity options, one single-stock futures contract will control 100 shares of stock and will trade through the third Friday of the expiration month.

Daily Price Limits

Even with marking to market, traders can get into large losses. To decrease the chances of that happening, most futures contracts have daily price limits. As stated earlier, this simply means that the underlying assets are allowed to only move up or down a certain amount per day before trading must be suspended, and that no trading can take place outside these limits on that day.

Daily price limits are normally set by the exchanges and can, under certain circumstances, be modified. For example, at the CBOT, corn futures are quoted in cents and quarter-cents per bushel and have daily price limits of 20 cents per bushel with no limit for the spot month (current month contract). If corn closed at 2.20 per bushel yesterday, the highest it could trade today would be 2.40 and the lowest it could trade would be 2.00.[7] If corn closes at 2.10 today, the new limits of 1.90 and 2.30 apply tomorrow.

Because each contract controls 5,000 bushels, the most you can gain or lose in a single day is 0.20 * 5,000 = $1,000. Most commodity futures contracts have daily price limits of some type and they vary in size based on volatility and size of the contract. Many futures contracts, however, do not have daily price limits, especially with the financial contracts such as bond or Fed funds futures.

If a contract trades at its upper limit, it is said to be *limit up* or *locked limit up*, emphasizing that trading is locked for the day. Likewise, if it reaches its lower limit, that contract is said to be *limit down* or *locked limit down*. The unnerving part about lock limit trading is that it can continue day after day, thus never allowing you a way out of the trade! So while the limits theoretically make it less risky, the reality is that you can still get stuck if a commodity decides to run away in price. For example, suppose that a commodity is trading at its upper limit, you are short the contract and will have losses at the end of the day. You wish to buy back the contract (an offsetting position) to get out. But if it is trading limit up, that signifies that people think the price of the commodity is going to move even higher — who do you suppose wants to sell? So while you may theoretically be able to buy or sell at or within the limits, the truth is you may not find someone to take the opposite side of the trade.

We'll show you in Chapter 6 how to protect yourself if you should find yourself on the wrong side of a commodity trade that is locked limit up or down.

The important thing to know is that SSFs will <u>not</u> have daily price limits! So while most of your daily gains and losses are expected to be small, if you get on the wrong side of a trade where the stock makes a large move, the losses can become large — quickly.

---

[7] The quote of 2.20 would probably appear as 2200 with the last digit representing the quarter-cents. We'll talk more about this in another section. For now, it's too confusing to use this notation to understand price limits.

There are certainly pros and cons to limit trading, and whether limit trading is generally good or bad for the markets is controversial. Incidentally, the minimum price fluctuation, called a *tick* size, will be one cent per share, or $1 per contract.

Key point:
Single-stock futures will <u>not</u> have daily price limits. This is a big difference from most commodity contracts, which often limit the daily amount the futures price is allowed to move.

Trading Hours

Single-stock futures will trade between 9:30 a.m. and 4:02 p.m. Eastern Time, which are the same hours as equity options. So while the underlying equities will stop trading at 4:00 p.m., the SSFs and options will continue for an additional two minutes. This may not seem like much time, but it can really help if you are trying to hedge a stock position going into the close. Many other financial futures contracts, such as the S&P 500 or Nasdaq 100 trade nearly 24 hours per day.

Delivery Process

As we've said earlier, most futures contracts are used for hedging or speculative purposes and are just closed in the open market with an offsetting position. However, if you do wish to buy or sell the actual stock, the standard trade date plus three-business-day settlement (T+3) will apply. If you take delivery through a futures contract, you will be long 100 shares per contract in three business days, and your account will be debited for the contract amount at that time, too. Because SSFs are not currently traded, it's difficult to say exactly what the procedure will be for taking delivery. The best thing to do is check with your broker regarding what they require, then just follow their procedures. Keep in mind that you cannot take delivery as with options. If you wish to acquire the actual shares by using your futures contract, you will need to wait until the third Friday of the expiration month.

On a technical note, if you are familiar with options, you are probably used to "exercising" your call option in order to take delivery of the shares. With futures contracts you do not exercise them. Exercising an option contract implies that you willingly decided to take delivery. With futures contracts you do not have that right. If you are long a futures contract, you simply do not close it out and automatically take delivery.

Settlement Day and Time

All futures contracts will "settle" at 10:00 a.m. on the following business day following the last trading day. What does this mean? It means that your *daily* gains, losses, and margin requirements will be calculated based on this amount. This is important to understand because the settlement price may be quite different from the last trade, which is used to determine margin requirements for stocks or short equity options.

For example, say you just entered a long Microsoft futures contract at $60. It is now the end of the trading day and the futures price closed up half a point at $60.50, which you would normally assume means you made a little money. More important, you don't owe any money. However, that closing price is irrelevant in futures trading and your gains or losses will be based on the settlement price, which is not determined until 10:00 a.m. the following morning.

It is possible that the stock is actually trading below that last trade at settlement time, which could bring your account below margin equity requirements. If so, you'll be required to send in more money even though the stock closed up.

The settlement price is determined by a settlement committee, which tries to determine the fair market value of that contract based at that time. There is usually a different settlement committee for each commodity. The proposed method for daily settlement of single-stock futures, according to the NQLX will be as follows:

Proposed Settlement Price Calculations

The Settlement System will calculate the Daily Settlement Price based on reported prices in the two-minute period prior to the time specified for contract settlement. The first 90 seconds of the settlement period will be used to monitor spread levels. The Settlement Price will be determined during the final 30 seconds of the settlement period, according to the following criteria:

a. A single traded price during the last 30 seconds will be the Settlement Price.

b. If more than one trade occurs during the last 30 seconds of the Settlement Range, the trade-weighted average of the prices, rounded to the nearest tick, will be the Settlement Price.

c. If no trade occurs during the last 30 seconds of the Settlement Range, the price midway between the active bids and offers at the time the settlement price is calculated, rounded to the nearest tick, will be the Settlement Price.

d. In the circumstances where there is no traded price nor updated bid/ask spread during the last 30 seconds of trading, the settlement price of that contract month shall be the settlement price of the first quarterly delivery month plus or minus the latest observed calendar spread differential between the first quarterly delivery month and the contract month in question. In the event that the relevant spread price differential is not readily observable, in order to identify appropriate settlement prices, Exchange Market Services may take into account the following criteria as applicable: 1) spread price differentials between other contract months of the same contract; and 2) price levels and/or spread price differentials in a related market.

Why do futures use a settlement committee to determine the fair market value rather than the last trade? In most cases, the settlement price will be equal to, or at least very close to, the closing price. However, there may be times when you may be holding an illiquid futures contract (not a lot of trading or open interest) and its price may not adjust quickly to current news. It is the job of the settlement committee to ensure, to the best of their ability, that all current information is being reflected in the price of the contract.

Each contract will have a symbol that indicates the settlement price determined by the committee. For instance, if you trade S&P 500 contracts, you can usually type in the symbol "SET" on many advanced quoting systems (as you would for getting quotes on a stock) and you will get the settlement price for the current contract. Similarly, "NQS" is usually the symbol for the daily settlement price for the Nasdaq 100. You will also be able to find the settlement prices for all contracts at each exchange's Web site.

While there are pros and cons to using settlement committees, it's not really a big concern one way or another. After all, a closing price is just a snapshot in time as is a settlement price. Sometimes the settlement price will be in your favor and other times it won't. It is not our intention to debate whether this method of settlement should or should not be used. Just be aware that is how it's done.

Chapter 4
Pricing of Futures Contracts

The previous chapter presented the basics of futures and how the settlement committee determines the settlement prices. The next question is: How are prices of futures contracts determined in general?

While other types of derivatives involve complex pricing formulas, futures contracts are relatively easy to price. Because we know today the price we've agreed to trade in the future, the value of that contract is nothing more than the current spot price plus the cost of carry, assuming the underlying asset provides no income (such as dividends) during the year. By cost of carry, we mean the interest you could earn on your money, which is also called the financing cost.

Now, with some commodities futures contracts, the cost of carry may be a little more difficult to determine. For example, a farmer may have to store grain for several months and then deliver it by rail. Additionally, he may have to buy insurance to guard against fire or water damage. In fact, it is not uncommon for regional differences in storage costs to cause different futures prices on different exchanges.

However, for financial assets, there are virtually no storage costs (the assets are held electronically) and the "shipping" costs are very low (they are sent through the Fed wire system), so the cost of carry is usually considered to be the only foregone interest.

For example, assume interest rates are 5%. If the underlying asset is currently trading for $100 and we enter an agreement to trade it for $100 in one year, we could replicate that futures contract by purchasing the asset for $100 today, holding on to it, and then delivering it for $100 in a year. In doing so, we would miss out on the interest we could have earned on the $100 we spent on the asset today. That amount would be $100 * 5% * 1 year = $5, so the futures contract should be worth $105. Remember, a futures contract is an *obligation* to buy or sell. If we buy the spot asset for $100 and sell a one-year futures contract at $105, we have guaranteed the sale of the underlying asset at $105, which is simply the initial cost of the underlying plus interest.

If the futures contract is not trading for $105, arbitrageurs will take advantage of the pricing discrepancy for a risk-free profit. For instance, assume the futures contract is priced at $106. We know it "should be" trading for $105 but we see it is not. The futures are overpriced in relation to the spot price. In this case, arbitrageurs would borrow $100 and owe $105 in one year. They will take the borrowed $100, buy the underlying asset in the spot market and hold on to it for one year. At expiration, they will deliver the asset for $106 and then repay the $105 loan, leaving them with a guaranteed $1 for no money at risk — an arbitrage profit. This is known as *cash-and-carry arbitrage* — the trader buys the spot asset (also called the cash market) and carries it to expiration.

Cash-and-carry arbitrage tends to raise the spot price and lower the futures price until the arbitrage opportunity disappears.

Instead, what if the futures were trading below $105, say $104? Now the futures contracts are too cheap compared to the spot price. Arbitrageurs would buy the underpriced futures at $104 and short the spot asset for $100. There is no cost to enter the futures contract, so the arbitrageur just puts the $100 credit in a risk-free interest account.[8]

Because the arbitrageur shorted the underlying asset, he now has the obligation to buy it back at some point in time — and there are no restrictions on the length of time. The arbitrageur is not at risk of paying higher prices like a typical short-seller, since he bought the futures contract and is guaranteed a purchase price of $104 in one year. The $100 credit grows to a value of $105 in one year, and he takes that money to buy the underlying asset for $104, leaving him an arbitrage profit of $1. Whenever the futures price is too low, arbitrageurs use *reverse cash-and-carry* arbitrage. Reverse cash-and-carry tends to lower the spot price and raise the futures price until the arbitrage opportunity disappears.

Notice how these two examples used one dollar above fair value and one dollar below fair value. We calculated fair value to be $105 and assumed futures prices of $106 and $104 respectively. As a

---

[8] The initial margin deposit is generally not considered a cost. That's because it is not a down payment but rather a good-faith deposit.

result, the arbitrage profits were $1 in both cases. The arbitrage profit is equal to the amount that the futures contract is mispriced above or below fair value.

So whether the futures price rises or falls below fair value, arbitrageurs will make a guaranteed profit. We can state fair value for assets that pay no dividends as a simple expression:

Futures fair value price = Spot price * (1 + interest rate)^{time}

where time is expressed in years or fractions of a year.

In our example, the spot price was $100, interest rates were 5% (which is .05 expressed as a decimal) and the holding period was one year. Using the above formula, the futures price should therefore be $100 * (1.05)^1 = $105, which is what we determined earlier.

If we assume the above contract is for a fraction of a year, such as six months, we just use the corresponding fraction as the exponent (the raised number) and the futures contract should be trading for:

Futures price = Spot price * $(1.05)^{1/2}$ = $102.50

Because we only need to hold the spot asset for 6 out of 12 months (half a year) we simply raise 1.05 to the 6/12, or 1/2 power. If we were holding it for 35 days, we'd simply raise 1.05 to 35/365.

There is an alternative method that is easier to do in your head. In this example, the investor would earn $5 interest on the $100 over the course of a full year. However, they are only out the interest over half a year so only will be compensated by half the amount, or $2.50. With this second method, just divide the interest rate by the fraction of a year it represents. For example, if you are using a three-month period, divide the interest rate by four since that is one-fourth of a year. If you are using 35 days, you would divide 365 by 35, which is 10.43. The two methods do not produce exactly the same answers, as the first method (using exponents) assumes compounding of interest. This alternative method is useful if you want to double-check your answers or to get close estimates in your head; however, the first method is the one used to produce the numbers you see and hear reported and is the one you should focus on.

When the futures contract is trading for exactly the cost of carry, it is said to be trading at *fair value*.

Figure 4.1 summarizes the two strategies:

Assumptions:
Spot price = $100
Fair value = $105
If futures are $106: Futures are too high, so buy spot and sell futures — cash-and-carry arbitrage:
Cash and carry arbitrage procedure:
1) Borrow $100 and owe $105 in one year.
2) Buy asset for $100 with borrowed funds and sell futures for $106.
3) Wait one year and deliver asset for $106.
4) Repay loan and profit by $106 - $105 = $1.
Effect: Raises the price of the underlying stock or index and lowers the price of the futures contract.
If futures are $104: Futures are too low, so buy futures and sell spot — reverse cash and carry arbitrage:
Arbitrage procedure:
1) Short spot and receive $100 credit with obligation to buy back short position at later time.
2) Invest $100 in risk-free account and buy futures at $104
3) Wait one year and replace borrowed asset by taking deliver of futures for arbitrage profit of $105 - $104 = $1.
Effect: Raises the price of the futures contract and lowers the price of the underlying stock or index.

Figure 4.1

The above argument holds true for any futures price above or below fair value. We can therefore say that the only futures price where no arbitrage can occur is at $105 — the fair value. Because arbitrage is a guaranteed profit for no cash outlay, you can be assured that arbitrageurs will keep the actual value of the futures contract very close to its theoretical fair value.

We have been assuming equal borrowing and lending rates in order to make these arbitrage opportunities work. For retail investors this is rarely the case, but it is often possible for many of the large brokerage and futures firms, which are precisely the ones carrying out the arbitrages. So while you may not be able to participate in the arbitrage profits, you should still take the time to understand the process. Arbitrage is important because it keeps prices fair for all of us.

It's also important to understand the meaning of fair value. You'll often hear the financial stations such as CNBC talking about it prior to market open, and many people place trades in the pre-market based on those indications. If you don't understand fair value, you may easily end up on the wrong side of the market.

Using Fair Value to Predict Market Direction at the Opening Bell

Advanced market traders will watch the futures trading to get an idea of whether the market will open up, down, or just sit flat. The two main indices used are the S&P 500 and the Nasdaq 100 futures contracts.

However, even advanced traders get confused by what exactly this futures quote means. They often associate the *change* in futures prices as the indication of the market open. For example, if the futures are trading up 20, many mistakenly believe this means a positive indication for the open. Likewise, they feel if the futures are trading down 10, that means the markets will open negatively. While this may appear to make sense, it is not necessarily correct; this erroneous interpretation can get you into trouble quickly if you are placing pre-market trades based on that misbelief.

When you hear CNBC and other financial sources talking about fair value, they are referring to the fair value of the S&P 500 index futures contract, which is widely regarded as the standard to gauge the overall markets. It is used by about 97% of U.S. money managers with more than $1 trillion in assets being pegged to that index. There are four contract months, each one being the last month of each respective quarter. The contracts are March (represented by the letter "H"), June (M), September (U) and December (Z).

Whenever you hear CNBC or other sources quoting fair value, they are always talking about the near-term contract.

The S&P 500 futures contracts, as we've stated before, are cash settled, which means you cannot take delivery of the underlying index. If you did, you would have to provide a portfolio of 500 stocks in the exact proportions of the S&P 500, which is rather tedious. But as we showed earlier, there's really no mathematical difference if a futures contract delivers the underlying asset or is closed out for cash. Settling the futures contract in cash is effectively the same thing as actually buying and selling the actual stocks in the index.

Because futures trade on separate markets from the spot market, they are subjected to their own sets of supply and demand, so they may wander off in different directions from the stock market. In fact, the futures trade all night long on GLOBEX, a computerized trading platform at the CME, from 4:45 p.m. until 9:15 a.m. Eastern Time. The U.S. stock market, however, doesn't open until 9:30 Eastern Time. This definitely leaves room for the two markets to get out of line from the theoretical cost of carry model we discussed previously. But if the futures get too far out of line, the arbitrageurs will correct for that at the opening bell.

Let's make some basic assumptions and then see how to calculate fair value:

- S&P 500 cash index (spot)   1150
- Interest rate   5%
- S&P 500 dividend yield   1.5%
- 75-day S&P futures   1162

The following formula is used to calculate fair value for stock index futures or any forward agreement where dividends or other cash forms are paid:

Fair value = Spot price * [1 + (interest rate - dividends)]$^{\text{days}/360}$

Notice how this formula is just a variation of the one we gave earlier, which is reprinted below:

$$\text{Fair value} = \text{Spot price} * (1 + \text{interest rate})^{\text{time}}$$

Rather than using "1 + interest rate" inside the parentheses in the basic formula, fair value for indexes that include dividends use the term "1 + (interest rate - dividends)," which is the *effective* interest rate. This is done to reflect the fact that your borrowing cost (interest rate) is reduced by money received (dividends).

With the above assumptions, we can calculate the fair value of this S&P futures contract, assuming we had to buy the value of the index and hold it to expiration:

Fair value of futures = 1150 [1 + (.05 - .015)]$^{75/365}$ = 1158.16

Based on our fair value calculation, the S&P futures "should be" trading for 1158.16. If they are, the index is said to be trading at "full carry." However, we see they are actually trading for 1162. Therefore, the futures are <u>overpriced</u> by 1162 - 1158.16 = 3.84 points. In this example, we would say the futures should be trading for a *premium* of 8.16 points above the current spot price of 1150, since the fair value calculation of 1158.16 is 8.16 points above that spot price. Rather than trading at the expected fair value premium of 8.16 points, the futures are trading at a premium of 12 points (1162 - 1150).

Because the futures are overpriced, we would expect to see arbitrageurs use cash and carry arbitrage. They will buy the under-priced stocks and carry them for future delivery by hedging with a short futures contract. In other words, they will buy the stocks representing the S&P 500 and sell the S&P 500 futures contracts. The short futures contracts guarantee the sale. This puts buying pressure on the stock market and therefore is an upward indication for stocks at the opening bell. The reason for the upward pressure is because the futures are trading above fair value.

Key point:
   If the futures are trading <u>above</u> fair value, it's a <u>positive</u> indication for stocks at the opening bell.

What if the futures were trading at 1152? We figured that fair value was 1158.16, so the futures are now too cheap. Arbitrageurs will attempt to short the stocks representing the S&P 500 and hedge by purchasing the futures contract (reverse cash and carry). These actions put selling pressure on stocks at the opening bell.

> **Key point:**
> If the futures are trading <u>below</u> fair value, it's a <u>negative</u> indication for stocks at the opening bell.

Here's where traders often get confused. Let's assume that yesterday the S&P 500 futures closed at 1168. This morning, prior to the stock market open, they are trading for 1162, down 6 points. Many traders think this means a negative indication for the market simply because the futures are down. However, even though they are down, they are still more than three points above the fair value of 1158.16, which is a positive indication for stocks at the open. Whether stocks are expected to rise or fall at the opening bell has <u>nothing</u> to do with whether the futures are up or down — it all depends on where the futures are trading *in relation to their fair value*. Because of the ease of arbitrage between stocks and futures, the futures contracts usually trade at close to full carry.

By the way, different sources may quote different fair values, but that does not mean a mistake has been made. Each firm calculating it has different borrowing costs and may have different assumptions about the compounding of interest; therefore each one will use a little different formula. Regardless, each firm attempts to answer these questions: How much does the spot asset cost, how long will I hold it, how much interest will I pay, and how much will I receive in dividends? Because fair value is a cost of carry calculation, that number changes just slightly on a daily basis. Each new day, fair value will be reduced slightly to reflect one less day's interest.

Market Imperfections

We just showed that arbitrage is theoretically possible if the futures contract is any amount above or below fair value. However, in the real world, there are many imperfections that make arbitrage impossible even though the futures contract may be trading outside of its theoretical cost of carry limit. Some of these imperfections are:

- Transaction costs

- Bid/Ask spreads
- Restrictions on short sales
- Different borrowing/lending rates
- Execution risk
- Lack of storability (for non-financial commodities)

Because of these imperfections, arbitrage opportunities may disappear even though the futures are not priced at their fair value. For example, let's say there is a 1% transaction cost (commission) to buy or sell the stocks representing the S&P 500. If so, our fair value calculation of roughly 1158 will no longer be the dividing point for arbitrage. Instead, a range of values will be created with no arbitrage being possible within this range.

Using the same assumptions as before, we can find that range. In order to successfully buy the S&P futures now, we must buy the spot asset plus a 1% commission, which increases the cost by a factor of 1.01. To buy the spot index, it will now cost:

$$1150 * 1.01 * 1.035^{75/365} = 1169.74,$$ which is approximately 1170

Note:
   To make the formula simpler, we're going to use the effective borrowing cost of 3.5%, which represents the 5% borrowing cost less 1.5% dividends.

In order to successfully buy the index and sell the futures for an arbitrage profit now, we must receive more than 1170 for the futures contract.

The transaction cost hurts us on the sell side as well. Because we will receive 1% less from a short sale of the stocks in the index, that results in losing 1%, which is the same as keeping 99% (0.99) of the proceeds.

If we sell the spot index, we will receive: $1150 * 0.99 = 1,138.50$ which will grow to a value of $1,138.50 * 1.035^{75/365} = 1146.58$ at expiration, which rounds down to 1146.[9]

---

[9] Technically, we would use a 5% cost of carry since we would not get to keep the dividends from a short sale. However, to keep the math easier, we're going to assume equal effective borrowing and lending costs.

In order to successfully sell the index for an arbitrage profit, we must pay less than 1146 for the futures contract. Prior to transaction costs, arbitrage was possible for any futures value above or below the fair value level of 1158. Now with the introduction of a 1% transaction cost, our fair value calculation is expanded to include a range of values where no arbitrage can occur. Specifically, if the futures trade between 1146 and 1170, arbitrage cannot take place.

Arbitrage will normally bring the futures prices inside this range rather quickly. If the futures are above 1170, arbitrageurs will buy the stocks and sell the futures, which tend to bring the futures price below 1170. If the futures fall below 1146, arbitrageurs then buy the futures and sell the stocks, which tend to bring the futures price back above 1146.

These arbitrageurs are usually using computer programs that analyze all opportunities by calculating the price on every stock in the S&P 500, as well as the current futures contract. Then they calculate fair value and enter the corresponding orders to carry out the appropriate arbitrage if one exists. This is known as *computer trading*, *program trading*, or simply *programs*. You may hear that term from time to time in the markets, as in the following excerpt from a 1992 Washington Post article:

> *Other traders said steep premiums of stock futures to stocks' cash value in late afternoon trading sparked computerized buy programs, after the Dow held a key level at 3240 during a sell-off. "We did not make a new low," that trader said. "Programs took the market up in the last hour."*

So there are many forces at work during the trading day on the stock and futures markets. Stocks are free to move independently of the futures but are still joined by the invisible force of arbitrage.

Using the Spread

We just showed that arbitrage would occur if the futures were either above or below 1170 or 1146 respectively. However, that's assuming that the spot index remained at 1150, which would almost never happen. If the futures are above 1170, they will be sold *at the same time the underlying asset is being purchased*. This means that whether cash-and-carry or reverse-cash-and-carry arbitrage is being used, both the underlying asset and futures will move in price. An invisible force ties the two assets together — one will not sit still while the other one moves.

What's more important for the arbitrageurs is the *difference* in value between the spot price and futures price, which is called the *spread* or *basis*:

Spread = Futures price - Spot price

Using the above example, computers would generate buy programs if the spread exceeds 20 (1170-1150) and the sell programs if they fall below -4 (1146-1150). Regardless of where the spot and futures prices are, their differences should not fall outside this invisible fence, otherwise arbitrage will occur. For example, your broker may tell you that "buy programs" are at 20 with "sell programs" at -4. This means that if the spread ever gets above 20 during the trading day, then the stock market will rise since buy programs will start.

While the true cost of carry will change with different levels of the spot market due to low risk-free rates and short terms to expiration for the futures contract, it usually will not have a large impact. For instance, assume the spot market rises from 1150 to 1160 during the day. Now the fair value is $1160 * 1.01 * 1.035^{75/365} = 1179.91$, which 19.91 points above the new cash price of 1160, which is still about 20 points, as we stated earlier. In this example, no matter where the spot index is trading, arbitrage will usually keep the spread under 20.

So the spread between the futures contract and the underlying index (the "cash" or "spot") is allowed to wander within this "invisible fence" around the fair value as shown in the Figure 4.2 below:

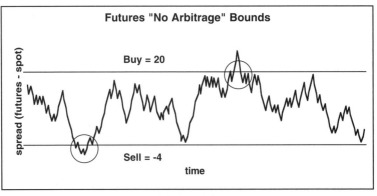

Figure 4.2

We can see that during this hypothetical time period that the spread actually fell below -4 (shown at the lower circled point) at which point the computer programs kicked in with the "sell programs." Now you may think that looks backwards since the line in the chart rises after that point, which looks like a buy program. However, the line in the chart represents the <u>spread</u> between the futures and the spot. When sell programs start, computers will sell stocks and buy futures (reverse-cash-and-carry), which <u>increases</u> the spread between the futures and the spot. Likewise, once the point at the upper circle was broken, the spread exceeded 20 and was too large. In other words, the futures became too expensive compared to the underlying stocks. Computers followed with cash-and-carry arbitrage and bought stocks and sold futures, which reduced the spread between them, which caused the line to fall. Just remember that the computerized trading is intended to keep the spread between the futures and the spot price within the fair value range. If the spread gets too wide, computerized trading will automatically reduce that spread. Likewise, if the spread gets too narrow, computerized trading will work to increase that spread.

So in relation to the stock market, the upper horizontal line at 20 represents "buy" programs and the lower line at -4 represents sell programs. The spreads gradually shrink as expiration nears since it costs less to finance the underlying asset with less time remaining.

Even though the arbitrage should theoretically bring prices inside these boundaries rather quickly, it's possible to stay outside the "buy" or "sell" ranges for extended periods of time, possibly hours at a time. If so, this happens because the futures markets are continually rising or falling at a <u>faster rate</u> than the spot market. If so, arbitrageurs cannot even bring the prices back in line quickly enough.

Key points:

It is the spread (difference between the futures and spot) that counts; it determines whether the "buy" or "sell" programs will start. If the spread gets too wide, buy programs will start (computers will buy stocks and sell futures) and the spread will narrow. If the spread gets too narrow, sell programs will start (computers will sell stocks and buy futures) and the spread will widen.

The concept of fair value is usually of little use for retail investors other than to satisfy their curiosity as to the direction of the market at the opening bell. Many investors get in trouble when they either buy or sell stocks in the pre-market (such as through Selectnet) based on the futures quote. Before you base your decisions on a futures quote, make sure you know where it is in relation to fair value. It is only then that you will truly know the expectation of the market at the opening bell. Also keep in mind that the effects of the arbitrageurs occur very quickly, and the stocks will get back "in line" with the futures prices usually within seconds.

There are occasions where this knowledge could benefit you greatly. Indices on futures also have price trading limits as do most commodities. If the futures trade at certain percentages above or below their closing price, then *trading curbs* may be put into place by the exchange. This is often known as a trading halt and is intended for investors to "take a breather" and think about their actions before jumping into the trading frenzy. For example, on the S&P 500 contracts at the CME, trading halts will occur during normal trading hours if that contract's price is 5%, 10%, and 20% below the prior settlement price. The lengths of the halts vary depending upon which percentage decline occurs. During after-hours sessions on GLOBEX, those same percentages apply for increases and decreases as well.

On October 19, 1987, "Black Monday," the S&P 500 was down more than 20%. Although the S&P 500 futures prices usually sell at a premium (higher price) to the spot index, they were actually below the spot price. Due to the heavy volume on that day, the New York Stock Exchange placed short-term restrictions on the way program trading could be done the following day. Because of these restrictions, program trading could not be carried out in the usual fashion, and the spread between the S&P 500 futures and the index slipped further. In fact, at its widest point, the futures contracts were trading at an 18% discount to the spot market. Had you known about fair value and program trading, you would have known to buy the S&P 500 futures contracts. Once the restrictions were removed, arbitrageurs and program traders would bid the futures prices to their normal level of spot price plus cost of carry — netting you a hefty profit along the way.

Questions

For the following questions, assume an index is trading for 1000, interest rates are 4% and no dividends are paid.

1) What is the fair value of a six-month futures contract on this index?

    a) 1040
    b) 1020
    c) 1004

2) If the spread reached 22 during this day, what would happen?

    a) Buy programs would start.
    b) Sell programs would start.

3) Explain how the actions in your answer to Question #2 would tend to bring prices back in line.

4) Yesterday the index closed at 1000 and the futures closed at 1127. However, this morning the futures are trading before market open for 1123, <u>down 4 points</u>. What is the expectation for stocks in this index at the open?

    a) Positive indication; stocks will be up at the open.
    b) Negative indication; stocks will be down at the open.

5) Your friend calls you before market open and claims he is going to place some pre-market trades on tech stocks since the Nasdaq 100 futures are trading <u>up 30 points</u> prior to the open. What should you tell him?

    a) Great idea; I'll do the same.
    b) We need to find out where fair value is before we can get a feel for how stocks will react.

6) You find out that the Nasdaq 100 index closed last night 40 points below fair value. What is the expectation for the Nasdaq at the open with their futures trading up 30 points?

    a) Positive indication; stocks will be up at the open.
    b) Negative indication; stocks will be down at the open.

Answers

1) What is the fair value of a six-month futures contract on this index?

b) 1020

1000 * (1.04) 6/12 = 1019.81 or approximately 20. You could perform this approximation in your head by knowing that 4% over one year would be 40 points, so half a year must be about 20.

2) If the spread reached 22 during this day, what would happen?

a) Buy programs would start.

If the spread is above the fair value of 20, then the futures are too expensive relative to the underlying stocks. Computer programs will buy the relatively cheap stocks and sell the relatively expensive futures contracts — cash and carry arbitrage or "buy" programs.

3) Explain how the actions in your answer to Question #2 would tend to bring prices back in line.

The computer programs will put buying pressure on the stocks and selling pressure on the futures contracts, which tends to reduce the spread.

4) Yesterday the index closed at 1000 and the futures closed at 1127. However, this morning the futures are trading for 1123 before market open, down 4 points. What is the expectation for stocks in this index at the open?

a) Positive indication; stocks will be up at the open.

Even though the futures are down, they are still 3 points above fair value level of 1120. This is a slight positive indication for the stocks at the open.

5) Your friend calls you before market open and claims he is going to place some pre-market trades on tech stocks since the Nasdaq 100 futures are trading up 30 points prior to the open. What should you tell him?

b) We need to find out where fair value is before we can get a feel for how stocks will react.

Remember, the net change in the futures contracts from one day to the next is meaningless unless you know where fair value is.

6) You find out that the Nasdaq 100 index closed last night 40 points below fair value. What is the expectation for the Nasdaq at the open with their futures trading up 30 points?

b) Negative indication; stocks will be down at the open.

Even though the futures are trading up at relatively high levels (+30), they are still 10 points below fair value. This is because they closed 40 points below fair value but are up 30 points through the night, which leaves them a net 10 points below. Computer programs will perform reverse-cash-and-carry arbitrage and continue to buy the relatively cheap futures and sell the relatively expensive stocks, which is a negative indication for the market.

Chapter 5
Understanding Futures Quotes

If you are trading futures contracts, you will obviously need to be able to read the quotes. They may look a little intimidating at first since many are quoted in cents rather than dollars, but they are actually quite easy once you understand the terminology.

In many ways, quotes on futures are not that different from quotes on stocks. You will see bids and offers, last trades, closing prices, highs and lows, and many other terms already familiar to you. For now, take a look at Figure 5.1, which shows the way futures quotes may be listed in your local paper or through your online broker:

GOLD (COMEX) 100 troy ounces; dollars per troy ounce								
Contract	Last	Chg	Open	High	Low	Settle	Lifetime High	Lifetime Low
April	300.9	-1.2	300.7	300.9	300.7	302.1	301.3	300.0
May	302.4	0.0	302.2	302.4	302.1	302.4	303.4	301.8
June	301.2	-1.7	302.6	302.9	300.7	302.9	303.5	300.1
August	301.6	-2.2	302.8	303.8	301.6	303.8	304.2	301.3

Figure 5.1

The heading in Figure 5.1 identifies the commodity, which is gold. The letters inside the parentheses designate the exchange at which the commodity is traded. This quote is from the Commodities Exchange (COMEX), which is a division of the New York Mercantile Exchange (NYMEX).

The second line in the heading provides the contract size, or the multiplier. We see that each contract controls 100 troy ounces and the quotes are in dollars per bushel. This is important information, since each commodity has a different multiplier and you need to know the size of the package before you can determine the total value of that package. Remember that single-stock futures will have a contract size of 100 shares per contract and will be quoted in dollars per share.

Below each heading will be the various contract months that are being traded. To reduce space we won't list them all here, but just be aware that the lists are often longer than just four months. Additional months will usually be designated by an abbreviated code for their month plus the last two digits of their expiration year.

If we look at the quotes under the column labeled "Last," we see that the April contract last traded at 300.9 dollars per troy ounce. That last price changed by $1.20 from the previous settlement price, which is shown in the "Chg" column. Because that number is negative, we know the price fell by $1.20. The "Open" column shows the where the contract opened the day for trading and the "High" and "Low" columns show the highest and lowest values that contract made during the trading day. The previous day's settlement price is shown under "Settle" and the "Lifetime High" and "Lifetime Low" columns tell us the all-time high and low prices for that contract since it first began trading.

Because each contract controls 100 troy ounces, a one-cent move is equal to $1 (.01 * 100 = $1). However, this contract just so happens to have a minimum price variation (tick size) of 10 cents, which simply means that 10 cents is the smallest increment the price is allowed to move. So while the commodity may theoretically be trading higher or lower at any given time, that price change will not register for this commodity until it is at least a change of 10 cents. Because of this minimum tick size, this gold contract will change in minimum increments of 100 troy ounces * 10 cents = $10.

From this information, we can also calculate the total contract value, which is 100 troy ounces * 300.9 = $30,900. Keep in mind that you only pay a small portion of this value, the initial margin, if you wish to enter this contract. At the time of this writing, the initial margin for that gold contract is only $1,350. For only $1,350 down, you immediately control $30,900 worth of gold based on these prices.

Other fields you may see printed, although not shown in Figure 5.1, are:

- Bid and Ask prices
- Volume (the number of contracts traded that day)
- Open interest (the total number of long positions or the total number of short positions in existence)

The bid and ask prices, as well as open interest, are important to understand if you are actively trading futures or options, so we'll go through both a little more in detail.

More About Bid and Ask Prices

If you have been investing at all, you are undoubtedly familiar with the bid and ask prices. The interpretation of the bid and ask in futures trading is exactly the same as for stocks, bonds, options and any other asset you may have traded. However, if you're a beginner, the bid and ask can be confusing and it's important to understand what they represent

If you look at the April contract in Figure 5.1, you will see the "last" trade is $300.90. This does not necessarily mean that is the current price, as the last trade could have been several minutes, days, or weeks ago. That is simply the price when it last traded. If you are about to place a trade on a futures contract, it is important to look at the bid or ask depending on whether you are buying or selling. Although they are not shown, let's assume the bid on this contract is $300.75 and the ask is $300.85.

The bid price is the price of the highest bidder; that is the highest price someone is willing to pay. The ask (also called the offer) is the lowest price among all the sellers. If this is confusing, just think about the terms you use when you buy or sell a house. If you wish to buy a house, you put in a bid for it. If you are selling your house, you tell a prospective buyer you are "asking" or "offering" it at a specific price. The same terms apply to financial markets. Just remember that bids represent buyers and asking prices (offer prices) represent sellers. Under normal market operating conditions, the bid price will always be the smaller of the two prices.

Why are only the highest bidder and lowest offer shown in a quote? Because they are the only prices that are ever of interest to the market. If you are selling your house, you're not concerned who will pay the least for it. If you were, you'd collect lots of $1 bids, $2 bids, and so on up the ladder. Anybody can bid low. Only the serious bidders will bid high. Likewise, if you are *buying* a house you're not concerned with who will charge the most for a given quality of home. If a certain quality home is going for $200,000, we're not concerned with the person who is willing to sell it for $300,000, $500,000, or even a million dollars. While high offers will always exist among any group of sellers, they are not of interest to the market. We want to know the prices of the highest bidder and lowest offer.

Notice how the highest bid and the lowest asking price create the smallest difference between the two prices, which is called the bid-ask spread. In our example, the bid-ask spread is 10 cents since that is the difference between the bid and ask of $300.75 and $300.85 respectively. The more competitive the market, the narrower the spread will become (assuming it meets the minimum bid increment). As you trade futures contracts, you will notice that most are highly liquid, which means lower prices if you are buying and higher prices if you are selling.

If you wish to buy a contract, you should look at the asking price, as that is the lowest price offered by the seller. If you are selling a contract, you should look at the bid, as that is the price submitted by the highest bidder. This does not mean that you must buy at the ask or sell at the bid any more than you should buy a house for the asking price or sell it to your first bidder. It does mean, however, that those prices are more relevant to your trade at that time and are better representations of value as opposed to the last price, high price, low price, or other prices you may see quoted.

The bid and ask prices are often a source of confusion for new traders since they are used to buying at the asking price and selling for the bid price. Because of this, they incorrectly think that the asking price represents buyers and the bid represents sellers. Upon closer examination, you should see that this is not possible. In order to trade a futures contract (or any product for that matter) you need a buyer matched with a seller. The reason you can buy at the asking price is because that person is a seller, so the trade can be matched and executed. Likewise, you can sell at the bid price since that bid price represents a buyer, which again matches the opposing sides of the trade and allows an execution.

To conserve space, the bid and ask prices are rarely shown in newspapers or other printed publications. However, if you are trading online or getting a quote from your broker, you can bet that you will see or hear the terms "bid" and "ask." You must be sure you understand what each one represents.

More About Open Interest

Open interest is a term unique to futures and options. It is simply defined as the total number of long or the total number of short positions. It is not the total number of long and short positions. That's because for every long position there must be a short position. Counting the total number of long and short positions would double-count them.

If you are familiar with options trading, you know that you must specify if a trade is either "opening" or "closing." With futures contracts, however, you do not need to specify whether your trade is opening or closing. That will be determined and reported by your brokerage firm. If you are entering into a contract, it will be reported as opening. If you are closing it by entering an offsetting position, it will be reported as closing. The clearinghouse will pair all "open" positions together; it is this number that is reported in "open interest." The fact that you do not need to specify "open" or "close" with each transaction really adds to the speed at which futures contracts can be used to change your directional bias. If you are long 10 contracts and now want to be short 10 contracts, you simply enter an order to sell 20 contracts. With options and stocks, you'd need to enter two separate orders, which we'll talk more about in Chapter 7.

Open interest does not necessarily change if you buy or sell contracts. It all depends on what the person on the opposite side of the trade is doing. For example, If I buy a contract to open and you sell a contract to open, then open interest will be increased by one. This is because both of us are opening. Likewise, if I sell to close and you buy to close, then open interest is decreased by one since both of us are closing. However, if I buy to open and you sell to close, then open interest remains unchanged.

Open interest is really just used so that traders have an idea of how many contracts currently exist and they can gauge the *liquidity* in that contract. The more investors in the contract, the more liquid and the more competitive the prices will be. Think about it as if you had a valuable painting you were taking to sell at an auction. Would you rather walk in and see a *couple* of people willing to buy or *several thousand* people? Obviously, you're more likely to sell for a higher price if there are thousands. What if, instead, you were going to *buy* a painting? Once again, you'd rather see many sellers, as you will likely get more competitive offers and a lower price. The same holds true for futures markets, which are nothing more than an auction. The more open interest, the more buyers and sellers there are and the more competitive are the prices, which means the bid and ask spreads will be narrow. This is useful information, because if you should need to exit the contract quickly, you would prefer to have high liquidity.

Be Careful with Commodity Quotes

Most commodity quotes are fairly straightforward to read. However, it's not a bad idea to check with your broker *before* entering the trade to make sure you understand the quotes. Some commodities have little quirks in the way they are quoted, and they can be misleading. For example, Figure 5.2 shows quotes from a wheat contract at the Chicago Board of Trade:

WHEAT (CBT) 5,000 bu.; cents per bushel								
Contract	Last	Chg	Open	High	Low	Settle	Lifetime High	Lifetime Low
May	2784	-36	2830	2840	2776	2822	3122	2522
July	2822	-32	2860	2874	2816	2854	3154	2554
September	2880	-24	2920	2932	2876	2904	3204	2604
December	2982	-26	3020	3030	2980	3010	3310	2710

Figure 5.2

We see that the May futures last traded at 2,784 cents per bushel, or at least that's how it appears. One may certainly think this means that the total contract value is 2,784 *cents*, or $27.84 per 5,000 bushels for a total of $139,200. However, it just so happens that wheat is quoted in cents and quarter cents per bushel and is a peculiarity among most of the grain contracts. The last digit, four, in the 2784 quote, is the number of quarter-cents, and is also the minimum tick size for this contract. One quarter-cent equals .0025 dollars and therefore one quarter-cent changes the value of this contract by 5,000 * .0025 = $12.50. In order to track changes of $100 increments, the exchange assumes this last digit is divided by eight. So a quote of 2784 is really $2.78 plus 4/8 of a cent or $2.785 cents per bushel for a total contract value of $2.785 * 5,000 = $13,925. If your broker quotes grains in this way, the last digit will always be a 0, 2, 4, or 6 with a zero representing an even move, a 2 representing 2/8 (1/4-cent move) and 6 representing 6/8 (3/4-cent move).

Again, the single-stock futures will be much more straightforward and quoted in straight dollars and cents per share. But peculiarities in quotes with other commodities are certainly something to be aware of if you ever decide to trade them.

Normal and Inverted Markets

Looking at the wheat quotes in Figure 5.2, notice how the "last" prices increase as the contract time is increased. In other words, as we move from May toward December, the prices of the contracts rise. For most commodities, this rising price pattern will often be the case, due to the cost of carry. Whenever you see this pattern of rising prices, that commodity is said to be in a *normal market*.

However, there are some commodities where the reverse pattern will be true. For instance, New York Harbor unleaded gasoline futures contracts at the New York Mercantile Exchange (NYMEX) are often cheaper as contract time is increased. This is called an *inverted market* and is shown in Figure 5.3:

Unleaded Gasoline (NYM) 42,000 U.S. gallons (1,000 bbls); cents per gallon								
Contract	Last	Chg	Open	High	Low	Settle	Lifetime High	Lifetime Low
May	.8100	-.0104	.8105	.8191	.8000	0.8204	.8220	.7982
June	.8030	-.0074	.8028	.8085	.7930	0.8104	.8106	.7912
July	.7810	-.0104	.7809	.7875	.7800	0.7914	.7830	.7784
August	.7635	-.0049	.7632	.7670	.7615	0.7684	.7652	.7595
September	.7404	0	.7400	.7434	.7390	0.7404	.7455	.7373

Figure 5.3

Then there are also some markets that are a mixture of normal and inverted markets that exhibit rising or falling prices for a few months but then reverse direction at some later point in time. For example, Figure 5.4 shows quotes on the oats futures at the CBOT, which follow the same 1/4-cent notation as the wheat contract:

OATS (CBT) 5,000 bu.; cents per bushel								
Contract	Last	Chg	Open	High	Low	Settle	Lifetime High	Lifetime Low
May	2010	+40	1962	2030	1956	1970	2170	1770
July	1732	+32	1696	1750	1692	1700	1900	1500
September	1440	+10	1434	1440	1430	1430	1630	1230
December	1436	+12	1430	1444	1430	1424	1624	1224
March 03	1460	+14	1460	1460	1460	1444	1644	1244

Figure 5.4

Looking at the prices in Figure 5.4 from May through December, we see that prices fall from 2.01 to 1.43-3/4 cents per bushel. However, from December through March of the following year, we see prices rise from $1.43-3/4 to $1.46 per bushel. This is a *mixed* market.

Why would prices rise in one market, fall in another, and be mixed in yet another? The answer lies in the net balance of the number of hedgers and speculators in that particular commodity. We said earlier that speculators provide an important economic function in the futures markets because they bear the risk. They are willing to take the opposing side of the hedgers and speculate on making money solely through price movements. There are a couple of strong theories that attempt to explain these rising and falling price patterns, which date back to the 1930s to the writings of two famous economists, John Hicks and John Maynard Keynes.

Hicks and Keynes supposed that some markets are dominated by long hedgers. These are markets where certain manufacturers wish to buy the underlying commodities in the future. In other words, they wish to lock in their future purchase price today. If these people wish to protect their purchase prices, they must persuade another person — usually a speculator — to take the short side of the futures contract. How do you persuade someone to hold a short futures contract? The long hedgers must bid it up *above* its expected spot price in the future. If they do, the price of the futures contract will fall as it nears expiration, leaving the speculator with a positive expected return.

For example, using our wheat quotes in Figure 5.2, let's say that everybody expects wheat to be trading for 2975 in December. If the futures markets price wheat exactly at this price, then a speculator who sells the futures contract today will be agreeing to sell wheat for 2975 in December. If the contract is, in fact, trading for 2975 in December, the speculator must buy it back at that same price, which leaves no net gain.[10] In other words, the speculator is agreeing to buy and sell wheat for 2975, which leaves no profit. However, if the long hedgers bid the contract up to a higher amount, such as 2982, the speculators can sell the contract for 2982 and buy it back for 2975 (remember that the futures price will converge to the spot price at expiration), which leaves them with an expected profit. Just because it is an *expected* gain does not mean that one will result. That is the incentive given by the long hedgers to get the speculators to take the short side of the futures contract.

While this may sound confusing, it is a natural occurrence whenever one person is trying to convince another to sell something. Take, for example, this story line from a *Seinfeld* episode:

> *George is invited over to his girlfriend's parent's house and brings a marble rye bread for them as a gift. George accidentally takes the bread he intended as a gift with him when he leaves. Jerry goes to the bakery to purchase a rye bread but discovers the last one has been sold. He offers the old lady that purchased the last one far more than she paid, but she refuses.*

Jerry was trying to get the lady to exchange the bread for money (a verbal contract). He wanted to be the buyer (the long position) so he had to give her incentive to be the seller — the short side of the contract. To provide this incentive, he keeps raising his bid price. At some point, at least theoretically, the lady should have realized she could purchase the bread at a later date for far less money and kept the rest as profit and agreed to sell. But theory didn't work for Jerry like it does for the futures markets.

---

[10]The speculator is technically not required to buy it back. However, if they do not, they must deliver the asset at expiration. Because speculators are not interested in making delivery, we assume they must buy back the contract.

In a similar sense, long hedgers with futures contracts must do the same thing. They must be willing to bid the contract higher than the price that is expected at expiration so that the seller, the short contract, can *expect* a profit. In a market dominated by long hedgers, we would expect the prices to continuously rise as time to maturity increases, which is exactly what we see with the prices of the wheat contracts in Figure 5.2.

The theory that says hedgers hold long contracts on a net balance is called the *contango* theory. Similarly, futures contracts that exhibit rising prices as time increases are said to be in a *contango* market.

Contango theory:
Hedgers hold long contracts on a net balance thus creating a normal market.

Contango market:
Futures markets that exhibit rising prices as time to maturity increases.

While prices rise from month to month in a contango market, the price of the contract is expected to fall as expiration approaches. This may seem contradictory, but think about what is happening. The hedgers must bid the contracts higher than their expected prices at expiration so the short sellers can expect a profit. So while the futures contract prices rise from month to month, the individual contract prices are expected to fall as expiration gets closer. Their prices fall because the futures price will converge to the spot price.

Figure 5.5 shows the mechanics of a contango market. The futures price is bid up higher than the current spot price and is also bid up higher than the expected spot price that will prevail in the future. Once that future spot price emerges, the futures price will fall to meet that price.

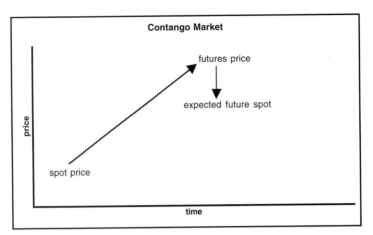

Figure 5.5

Please keep in mind this is a theory that explains this price pattern. It does not necessarily mean that it must turn out this way. Nonetheless, we should expect to see an overall positive return for short sellers of futures contracts in a contango market.

We've just seen why some markets exhibit rising futures prices as the time to maturity increases. How can we explain patterns of falling prices such as in Figure 5.3 with unleaded gasoline?

There is a theory opposite that of the contango theory which states that some markets will be dominated by short hedgers — those wishing to sell the asset in the future. These people are usually the producers of the commodity who wish to protect their selling price and therefore need a short hedge. In order to persuade a specu-lator to hold a long futures contract in this market, the hedgers must sell it below the expected future spot price so that the speculator can expect a positive return.

This is probably confusing at first, so let's use another example you're more familiar with. Let's say you wish to trade in a car that has a market value of $10,000. That's the price it can be sold for quickly at a retail dealership. If that were the case, why would the dealer give you $10,000 for it? If he did, he would pay $10,000 for the car and then sell it for the same amount, which leaves him with no profit. In order to persuade the dealer to take your car (take the long position), you must be willing to take less than the market value for it (although the ridiculously low bids made from the dealer are another story!). You may, for example, take $8,500 for it, meaning the car dealer is "long" at $8,500 and can sell it for the expected $10,000 market value, which leaves him an expected profit.

In the same sense, short hedgers must be willing to take less than the expected future spot price to get a speculator to hold the long side of the futures contract. The theory that supports this argument is called *normal backwardation* and, just for the record, I had nothing to do with the selection of that term! At any rate, normal backwardation theory states that hedgers are primarily short the futures contracts and speculators are long. The short hedgers compete in the market and push the price below the expected future spot price in order to get a speculator to purchase the contract.

Normal backwardation theory

Hedgers hold short contracts on a net balance thus creating inverted markets.

Normal backwardated market

Futures markets that exhibit falling prices as time to maturity increases.

Figure 5.6 shows how the dominant short hedgers push the futures prices below the expected future spot price. This below-expected price allows the speculators to expect a positive gain. Again, please do not think that if you hold long futures contracts that you must have a gain. This theory suggests that the overall price is below what it is expected so that the long speculators have some incentive to hold the contract. Market conditions can change quickly, leaving the long positions with large losses. So the theory suggests that one can expect a positive gain over time and not that gains must occur on each contract.

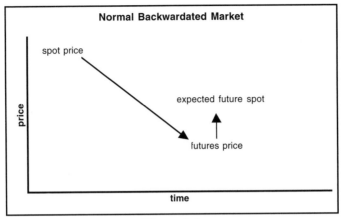

Figure 5.6

Other markets such our oats example in Figure 5.4 exhibit a mixed market whereby sometimes the prices rise (or fall) throughout a certain range and then reverse directions at a later time. The rational for the mixed markets is basically a mixture of the contango and normal backwardation theories. Depending on supply and demand conditions, sometimes the markets are dominated by long hedgers and other times by short hedgers. Harvests also affect the supply side and can cause prices to fall when crops are expected to come to market in large quantities.

So while contango markets rise in price with the more distant months, those prices are expected to fall as expiration nears to compensate the short speculators. The reverse is true for normal backwardated markets. Normal backwardated markets fall in price with the more distant months; however, those prices are expected to rise as expiration nears to compensate the long speculators. Figure 5.7 shows how contango markets are expected to fall and normal backwardated markets are expected to rise as expiration nears:

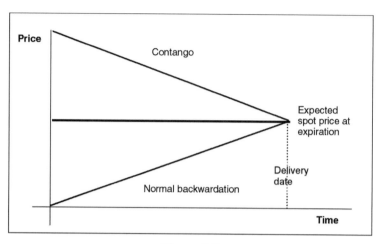

Figure 5.7

More on Price Discovery

We have just seen how futures prices can provide a means for investors to "see into the future" and gauge where prices are expected to be trading. We referred to this earlier as price discovery. We now need to take a little closer look at different market types and to learn why price discovery may work well in some markets while not so well in others.

While there are many types of futures contracts, they can basically be categorized as either a "storable" commodity or a "non-storable" one. Most grains such as wheat, oats, and rice, for example, are storable and can be preserved for long periods of time. Others such as milk or eggs cannot be stored for a long length of time. These are the "non-storable" goods.

The non-storable commodities are what provide the most efficient means of price discovery. That is, the futures price is a pure reflection of what market participants expect the future price of that commodity to be. If the supply of milk, for example, were expected to rise in the next three months, you would see the futures prices rise to that expected level as well. In a storable goods market, this may not be the case. The reason you may not see futures prices of non-storable goods rise under the same conditions is that market participants can pull that supply out of the market today and store it for delivery in the future. This is similar to our "cash-and-carry" arbitrage we talked about in Chapter 4. For example, if wheat is expected to rise 20% in the next three months, you still may not see that much of a difference between the spot price and the futures price. That's because as the price of the futures contracts rise, arbitrageurs will buy wheat today, store it, and deliver it in the future. These actions will put buying pressure on the spot price and selling pressure on the futures price. You will see a rise in the spot price rather than a rise in the futures price. The end result will be that the spot price and futures price will be separated by the cost of carry.

If the commodity is not storable, or at least not easily stored, then arbitrageurs will not be able to complete the cash-and-carry arbitrage steps. They cannot buy that future supply today because it does not exist, and they certainly cannot store it. The result is that the futures price must fully reflect that change in expectations.

You may hear news sources say something like, "The futures markets are pricing an anticipated quarter-point rate hike from the Feds." This simply means they are looking at the Federal Funds futures contracts and observing the difference between that price and the current rate. The Federal Funds futures are a good predictor of future rates; they behave like a "non-storable" commodity, since you cannot meet future bank reserves by purchasing them today. For storable commodities, such as wheat, the futures may not serve as a good predictor of the expected price due to the fact that arbitrageurs can buy it today and store it for future delivery.

So be careful when using futures quotes as a predictor for future prices. Only when the commodities are non-storable will the futures markets serve as a valuable predictor of future prices.

Questions

1) A single-stock futures contract is quoting a price of $35. What is the total contract value? How much is the initial margin at 20%?

2) A wheat futures contract is quoted in cents and quarter-cents per bushel and controls 5,000 bushels per contract. What is the total contract value if the quote is 3,004?

3) You are looking at quotes and observe that the prices rise as contract maturity increases. What type of market is this?

    a) Normal market
    b) Inverted market
    c) Backwardated market

4) You are looking at quotes and observe that the prices fall as contract maturity increases. What type of market is this?

    a) Normal market
    b) Inverted market
    c) Mixed market

5) You are about to look up some quotes on a commodity that you suspect is dominated by long hedgers. Would you expect to see prices rise or fall as maturity increases?

    a) Rise
    b) Fall

6) You are about to look up some quotes on a commodity that you suspect is dominated by short hedgers. Would you expect to see prices rise or fall as maturity increases?

    a) Rise
    b) Fall

7) Your broker tells you that a particular commodity is in contango. Will the farther months be more or less expensive than the near-term months?

8) A futures contract is bid $22.30 and asking $22.50. The price you can currently buy this contract for is:

a) $22.30
b) $22.50
c) $22.40
d) You cannot buy a contract if there is a bid and ask.

9) What does the bid price represent?

a) The price of the buyer willing to pay the most
b) The price of the buyer willing to pay the least
c) The price of the seller asking the most
d) The price of the seller asking the least

10) The open interest of a particular futures contract is 100. You buy 10 contracts today and are the only volume for the day. You notice that the open interest is still 100 tomorrow rather than the 110 you expected. How would you explain this?

a) The trade opposite of you must have been closing a position.
b) A mistake in reporting has obviously been made.
c) Open interest is just an approximation.

Answers

1) A single-stock futures contract is quoting a price of $35. What is the total contract value? How much is the initial margin at 20%?

Each contract controls 100 shares of stock, so the total contract value would be 100 * $35 = $3,500. The initial margin deposit would be $3,500 * 0.20 = $700.

2) A wheat futures contract is quoted in cents and quarter cents per bushel and controls 5,000 bushels per contract. What is the total contract value if the quote is 3,004?

The total contract value would be 300.5 cents * 5,000 = $15,025. Remember that the last digit is divided by eight, so the quote is for 300 cents plus 4/8 cents, which is 300.5 cents.

3) You are looking at quotes and observe that the prices rise as contract maturity increases. What type of market is this?

a) Normal market

4) You are looking at quotes and observe that the prices fall as contract maturity increases. What type of market is this?

b) Inverted market

5) You are about to look up some quotes on a commodity that you suspect is dominated by long hedgers. Would you expect to see prices rise or fall as maturity increases?

a) Rise

6) You are about to look up some quotes on a commodity that you suspect is dominated by short hedgers. Would you expect to see prices rise or fall as maturity increases?

b) Fall

7) Your broker tells you that a particular commodity is in contango. Will the farther months be more or less expensive than the near-term months?

More expensive

8) A futures contract is bid $22.30 and asking $22.50. The price you can currently buy this contract for is:

b) $22.50

9) What does the bid price represent?

a) The price of the buyer willing to pay the most

10) The open interest of a particular futures contract is 100. You buy 10 contracts today and are the only volume for the day. You notice that the open interest is still 100 tomorrow rather than the 110 you expected. How would you explain this?

a) The trade opposite of you must have been closing a position.

Chapter 6
The Trading Process on Single-Stock Futures

We've covered a lot on futures, so let's review the previous topics by using an example. However, we're going to start at the very beginning from opening an account through opening and closing your first trade.

Currently, if you wish to trade futures, you must do so through a futures broker, which is technically called a Futures Commission Merchant, or FCM. If you invest in stocks, you buy and sell from a broker; if you invest in futures, you buy and sell from an FCM. However, once single-stock futures (SSFs) begin trading, you will be able to place trades on those contracts through either a broker or FCM, which will make the process a whole lot easier since you won't have to open separate accounts. This is because SSFs aren't easily classified into a futures or stock products. The CFMA said these hybrid products should be treated as both and therefore regulated by the Securities and Exchange Commission (SEC) and the Commodity Futures Trading Commission (CFTC). Therefore, any firm trading SSFs must be registered as a broker dealer with the SEC and as a futures commission merchant with the CFTC. Keep in mind that this applies only to SSFs. If you wish to trade commodity futures, you must do so through an FCM.

Opening an Account

Opening a futures trading account is very easy, and the process is not much different from opening a stock trading account. First, the broker will require you to fill out an account application. These are generally three to five pages long with basic information including past investment experience. Additionally, there will be a confidential net worth statement, which is required by law under the "know your customer" rule. The brokers need to know that you have a positive net worth before you invest in futures. You will also need to sign a supplemental risk disclosure document that states you have read and understand the risks involved in futures trading.

Most FCMs will e-mail or fax an application to you, but they cannot accept an e-mailed or faxed signature. However, the better firms usually provide their Federal Express account number so you can overnight the application back to them at no cost to you.

Placing an Order

Once you open your account, you're ready to take advantage of single-stock futures. Let's assume it is January and Microsoft is trading for $60. You think the stock price will rise over the next three months and wish to buy a futures contract.

You simply call your broker and give him the instructions to buy one Microsoft March futures contract. Remember from Chapter 5 that we are initiating this position, so we are "opening" and when the time comes to exit the position, we would be "closing," although we do not need to specify the terms "opening" or "closing" when placing the order. However, some brokers may use the terms just to confirm what you are doing so there are no mistakes. For example, they may say, "Is this an opening contract?" or something to that effect. Incidentally, because many new traders find this terminology confusing, some brokers will use the terms "new" and "offsetting" to designate opening and closing transactions respectively.

The broker will give you the contract symbol, which, according to the Securities Industry Association (SIA), will likely be a five-letter code representing the underlying stock followed by a standardized letter representing the month. Figure 6.1 gives the standard codes for the months for all futures contracts:

Month Code	Month
F	January
G	February
H	March
J	April
K	May
M	June
N	July
Q	August
U	September
V	October
X	November
Z	December

Figure 6.1

A proposed symbol structure by the SIA for single-stock futures will look something like Figure 6.2:

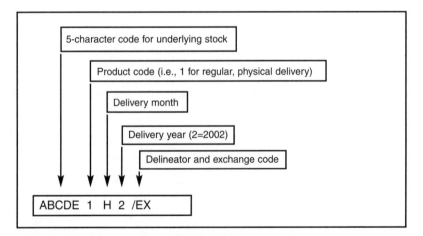

Figure 6.2

The proposed symbols will not be a nice, simple three- or four-letter code that you're used to seeing with stocks. That's because there has not been any formal arrangement between futures and equities regarding symbols. In fact, there are currently some symbols that are the same for futures and stocks and must be separated by an exchange code at the end. With the development of SSFs, there could certainly be room for complications if these measures were not taken. Unfortunately, awkward symbols will be the result. There's no need to worry about it, as your broker will certainly look up the symbol for you.

Let's assume the broker tells you that the March contract on Microsoft is trading for $61. Because each futures contract represents 100 shares of stock, that contract has a value of $6,100. Of course, you will only be required to post the initial margin, which is expected to be 20% of this value, or $1,220. We're also going to assume that maintenance level will be 20% below this amount, or $976.

Once you get the symbol for your contract, you will need to give the broker your order. To do so, you will need to tell him the following information:

- Action (buy or sell)
- Quantity (number of contracts)
- Contract (name of contract, i.e. Microsoft, Intel, S&P 500)
- Month (expiration month)
- **Price** (market or limit — *see below*)
- **Time** (How long do you want the order to stay open? *See below*)
- Exchange (To which exchange do you want your order to go?)

Your broker will be able to help you with most of the information. However, when it comes time to decide on price and time, you must supply that information, so it is important to understand the following types of orders. While the following is a fairly extensive list, it is not exhaustive. But it does contain most of the orders used in nearly all of the cases you will ever need to use. Also, just because these orders exist does not mean that your broker must offer them. Be sure to investigate which types of orders they accept.

To place the order, we need to tell the broker to buy one Microsoft March contract. In most futures markets, the number of contracts will be straightforward with the exception of grains and soybeans. In those commodities, because the contract size is 5,000 bushels, it is conventional to just strike three zeros off the contract size to determine the number of contracts. For example, if you tell your broker to buy five corn contracts, you are really just purchasing one contract, which controls 5,000 bushels. This really shows that it is important to confirm the order with your broker. You can see where trading lingo and other oddities within each marker can really cause confusion.

We're going to place our hypothetical Microsoft trade "at market" to be sure we get filled. If you are familiar with what this means and are comfortable with the various types of orders, you can skip to the next section, "Confirming Your Order," and continue with the example. However, if you are not familiar with them, or just wish to take a quick review, most of the types of orders you will encounter are listed below:

Types of Orders

Most of the orders you're used to seeing with stocks, such as market, limit, stop orders, and others will apply to futures as well. Additionally, there are some types of orders that are unique to futures. We'll go through each to make sure you understand the basic ideas behind them.

Orders That Control Price: Market, Limit, Opening Only, Market on Open, Or-Better, Disregard Tape

The most commonly used orders for buying and selling contracts are *market* and *limit* orders. Depending on your situation, one order will be preferable to another, so it is important to understand the differences and risks with each type.

Market Orders

Let's start with the most important feature of a market order, which is that <u>market orders guarantee the execution but not the price</u>.

In fact, a market order is the only way to make certain you will get the trade executed.[11] However, in order to do guarantee the fill,

---

[11] The only exception is with stocks since a short sale must be executed on an uptick and there is no guarantee that will occur. Remember that futures do not need an uptick to go short, so market orders guarantee an immediate fill on a long or short futures position.

you must be willing to accept the best available price at the time your order hits the floor. So while you may see a contract quoting a certain price when you send your order, that is not necessarily the price at which you will be filled. In most cases, though, it will be very close if not exact. Also, be sure to look at the *current* asking price if buying (or the current bid price if selling) rather than the last trade. That last trade could have taken place a long time ago and might not accurately reflect the true price of the contract.

There are also times when fast markets occur, which means the quotes are not keeping up with the true order flow. In these cases, you may certainly be filled at an unfavorable price, and you will have no recourse with your broker. Be careful using market orders under "fast market" conditions.

Two Special Cases of Market Orders: Opening Only, Market on Open

There are two special cases of market orders you should be aware of. They are "opening only" orders and "market on open." Both of these are types of market orders, as they are guaranteed to fill; however, they specify *when* the order is to be filled.

Opening-Only Orders

An opening-only order can only be filled during the opening range of prices. If the order is a market order, it must be filled. If it is marked as a limit, stop (or stop limit) then it may or may not be filled. Many traders elect to use this type of order because they feel this range of prices is a truer representation of value than intraday prices.

Market on Open (MOO)

This type of order is used to execute trades at the opening. Traders often use this designation to take advantage of a buildup of sell or buy orders through the night. For instance, if you wish to sell your contract and good news is released near the close of trading, you may wish to enter a MOO order for the following day. That way, you will likely get a higher price from the influx of buy orders that arrive through the night.

Limit Orders

While market orders have the advantage of a guaranteed fill, they come with the disadvantage of not necessarily knowing the price you will pay or receive. Limit orders were developed to prevent this risk.

With a limit order, you tell your broker that you are willing to buy or sell but only at a certain price, which is called the limit price. If you say to buy the March Microsoft futures contract at a limit of $60, this means your order will only be filled if it can be filled for $60 *or less*. If you wish to sell at a limit of $60, that means your order will only be filled if it can be filled for $60 or more. Because you are specifying a specific price, the risk of the limit order is that your order will never get filled. Limit orders guarantee the price but not the execution.

Also, a limit order may be filled in part, unlike a market order. For example, if you place an order to buy 10 contracts at a limit of $60, it's possible that you get filled on only five contracts or some other number less than 10. With a limit order, what you are really telling your broker is that you are willing to buy *up to* 10 contracts. If you are only willing to buy all 10 or nothing at all, you will need to use an "all-or-none" restriction discussed later.[12]

When placing an order, you need to figure out which is more important — making sure it is filled (market orders) or making sure you get a certain price (limit orders). There is no way to guarantee the execution *and* price — you get one or the other.

Or-Better Orders

There is a type of limit order which sort of blends a market and limit order called an "or better" qualifier. With an or-better order, you place buy orders above the current asking price and sell orders below the current bid price. Why would anyone be willing to pay a higher price or receive a lower price? It allows some room for the contract's price to move while your order is being routed to the floor.

---

[12]This is not necessary with the equity options markets, as all option quotes must be good for at least 20 contracts. However, this is not the case for futures contracts; a particular quote may only be good for one contract.

Assume that Microsoft contract is asking $60.75. You could tell your broker to buy the contract at a limit of $61 *or better*, for example. Now, when your order hits the exchange floor, you will be filled as long as it doesn't exceed $61. Some people think this is a recipe for disaster, as the floor will probably fill you at the higher $61 price. This is not true, as the traders are bound by time and sales, which reflect the current prices at the time your order was received. With or-better orders, your order is still not guaranteed to fill but the odds are much higher compared to a straight limit order. Assuming you're willing to pay the higher price, I would almost always use "or better" orders if the underlying stock is moving quickly.

DRT Orders (Disregard Tape)

A DRT order is a discretionary order that allows the brokers to use their judgment in obtaining a better price. This does not mean they will be able to get you a better price; in fact, you may even get a worse price. However, in most cases, if you consistently use these orders, you should obtain slightly better fills over the long run. This is because the brokers on the floor have much more knowledge than most investors do as to what is happening down there. A DRT designation gives them discretion to use their expertise in *trying* to obtain a better price.

DRT orders are more commonly known as a "not held" or "market not held" order when dealing with stocks. All of these orders accomplish the same thing and are basically saying that you will not hold the broker to the time and sales reports (the tape) if you should get an unfavorable price.

For example, if you place an order to sell your contract at market DRT, you may see prices over the next several minutes of $62 or higher trading. However, you may get a confirmation back with a fill at $61.90. You cannot come back and tell your broker you saw higher prices and are therefore due a better price. They will come back and tell you that the ticket was market DRT, which gives full discretion to the floor broker and there is nothing that can be done.

While this may not be a complete list of all of the orders, it will be nearly all you'll ever need to know. Keep in mind that as financial innovations reshape the markets, new types of orders will inevitably be introduced.

Orders That Control Risk: Stop, Stop Limit, Market-If-Touched, Market-on-Close

Stop and stop limit orders are intended to be risk-management tools. They are usually used as a means to sell an exit an existing position if unfavorable price movements occur. In other words, they are used to sell long positions and buy back short positions. While stop and stop limit orders can really help you, they can also cause great losses if you're not sure how they work.

If you are planning to use stop orders on your futures trades, make sure you understand this section.

There are two basic types of stop orders: *stop orders* and *stop limit orders*. There are very important differences between the two, so we'll look at them individually.

Stop Order

A stop order is a conditional order to buy or sell at market. You specify a price at which point the trade is "triggered" and becomes a market order to either buy or sell.

For example, say you paid $60 for the futures contract and it is now trading for $70. You feel it could climb much higher so you'd like to keep holding it, but at the same time you don't want to see it fall back to $60. This is the ideal situation for a stop order. You could place an order to sell your contract at a stop price of $68, for example. When you specify a stop price, that is the "trigger price" and is not necessarily the price you will get for your contract. So if the contract trades at $68 or *lower*, your order is triggered and becomes a market order, which will be filled at the next best available price.

It is very important to note that the contract needs to trade at or lower than your stop price in order to become triggered. This is where a lot of traders get themselves in trouble. Using the above example, say you placed a stop at $68 and the contract settles that day at $68.50. The stop order is not triggered, so at this point you still have the contract. However, the first trade the following morning is $62 on bad news. Because the last trade is below the stop price of $68, you will be filled at market — around $62 — which is very different from the stop price of $68. Remember, the stop price is only a trigger point and is the price where the order is activated. It is not necessarily the price you will receive! In cases where the futures contract falls slowly, though, stop orders work very well and the price you receive can be close to your stop price.

Stop orders used to be called "stop loss" orders until the Securities and Exchange Commission ruled to change the name because it was misleading. It sounds like the order will prevent losses, which is definitely not true.

Stop Limit Orders

In the last example we assumed you placed a stop order of $68 in anticipation of getting that amount if the contract should fall. Under normal circumstances, if the contract falls slowly, this method can work great. It's only when you see the large gaps down where the prices can be very different.

What if the there is a large gap down but you would rather hold on to your contract if you can't be assured of getting the $68 stop price? This is the ideal situation for stop limit orders.

With a stop limit order, you specify two prices. One is the trigger point and the other is the sell limit price. If you'd rather hold the contract in case you can't sell for $68, you could instead place a stop limit order and tell your broker to sell at a stop price of $68 with a stop limit of $67.50. If the stock trades at $68 or below (the stop price) the order will be activated as with a regular stop order. However, instead of becoming a market order, a stop limit order becomes a limit order to sell. This order says to activate it at $68 (the stop price) but do not sell for anything less than $67.50 (the limit price). The limit price can be equal to or less than the stop price.

In this example, when the futures contract opened at $62, the trader with the stop limit order would also have their order activated. However, they will still hold the contract because it could not be sold for $67.50 or higher. If the stock does rise to that price during the day (or later if a good-'til-cancelled order), the contract will be sold. *Remember, it is a live order once it has been triggered.* If you do not want to sell the contract, you need to cancel the order.

Notice again that the stop limit order did not prevent a loss either when the futures price gapped down below the stop limit price. With the stop limit order, you still own the contract. The stop order just gives a realized loss, since it is sold, while the stop limit order gives an unrealized loss.

Buy Stops

Buy stops work the same as sell stops but in the other direction. Usually they are used by short sellers — those who borrow shares to sell hoping to buy them back cheaper at a later time. In order to prevent the futures price from getting away from them to the upside, these traders often place buy stops.

For example, say you are short the Microsoft contract at $60. The risk to this trader is that Microsoft moves higher. In order to make sure the stock doesn't get away from you, you could place a buy stop at $62. This means you buy the shares at market if the futures trade at $62 or higher. Again, this is not necessarily the price you will pay, as the $62 in this example is only the trigger point.

If the trader does not want to pay more than a certain price, he can elect to place a buy stop limit. As an example, you could place an order to buy the futures at a stop price of $61, with a stop limit of $61.50. If the futures trade at $61 or higher, the order will be activated but will only fill if the contracts can be purchased for $61.50 or lower.

Traders also use buy stops to buy contracts on momentum. For example, say Microsoft stock has been sitting flat for a very long time at $60. The rumor is that a new product is expected to be released that could send the shares much higher. Rather than buy it now and possibly wait a long time for that day to come, traders may put in a buy stop order at $63 (and possibly add a stop limit), for example. Now, the only time the trader will be filled is if the futures contract is trading at $63 or higher. In effect, the trader is buying the stock only if it appears the market is starting to rally the stock. Again, this is a nice management tool to assure that you purchase the contracts on anticipated news without having to watch the markets all day long.

Market-If-Touched (MIT)

Market-if-touched orders, also called *board orders*, are unique to futures trading. You will not be able to use them for stock or options trading, although that may change in the near future. A market-if-touched (MIT) order is like a reverse stop order. It allows a trader to buy or sell if the price moves in a favorable direction, rather than an unfavorable one. For instance, if you buy the Microsoft contract for $60, you may wish to sell if it hits $65. Normally, you would have to use a sell limit order and place an order to sell your contract at a limit of $65. The problem with this type of order is that you must receive *at least* $65 in order to get filled. An MIT order at $65, however, will trigger if the contract touches (trades at) $65 or higher. Once it does, the order becomes a *live market order* and sells your contract at the best prevailing price at the time your order is filled, which may be below $65. If the market reverses directions quickly, you may not be able to get filled with a sell limit of $65 but would get out with an MIT order.

Notice how this order differs from the sell-stop where you may place an order to sell at a stop price of $58, for example, which is an unfavorable move. Both the MIT and stop orders get you out of the contract. However, the MIT does so on a *favorable* move while the stop order executes on an *unfavorable* one. The MIT order is used to lock in gains while a stop order is used to minimize losses.

MIT orders can be used to close short futures contracts as well. In this case, you simply place the order to buy the contract at a lower price.

Market on Close (MOC)

There exists a very useful tool that's not widely used by most traders. It's called a market-on-close order or MOC. With an MOC order, you try to buy or sell your contracts at a limit price during the trading day. If it is not filled, it converts to a market order within the final seconds of trading (60 seconds for financial futures). A market on close order must be filled within the prices that occurred during these time frames.

For example, say you bought two contracts at $60 and they are now selling for $70. The market looks really strong and there is a possibility it could trade much higher. However, you don't want to lose your profit. You could place an order to sell your two contracts at a limit of $72 MOC. Now, if it trades at $72 or higher, you will be filled. But if it doesn't trade that high, you will be sold very close to the closing price of the day. Keep in mind this could be much less than you anticipated! But MOC orders can be a great tool, as they allow you to try for better prices during the day but are assured to execute your order by the end of the day regardless. Please keep in mind that many brokers will refuse this order if it is not placed during a specified period (usually at least 15 minutes) before the close of trading.

Time Limits:
Day, Good-Until-Cancelled, Immediate-or-Cancel, Fill-or-Kill

If you use any order other than a market order, you must also specify a time period that the order is to remain open. Remember, a market order is guaranteed to fill so it can only be marked as a day order (even though it will usually be filled within seconds). Technically there are four different time designations:

- Day
- Good-until-cancelled (GTC)
- Immediate-or-cancel (IOC)
- Fill-or-kill (FOK)

By far, most trades are entered as either day or good-until-cancelled, but we will go over each one so you understand them all.

If you enter an order other than "market" it is not guaranteed to fill, so your broker will need to know if you want the order cancelled at the end of the day (day order) or cancelled after an indefinite time period with a good-'til-cancelled order, also called GTC. However, individual firms are free to set stricter requirements so may not allow a GTC order to stand open until the contract expires, so you should check with your broker as to their policy. In fact, at the time of this writing, the New York Board of Trade only allows day orders due to the September 11 attacks, which damaged their trading floors; they are now unable to hold tickets overnight. This is just to point out that GTC orders may vary from firm to firm and may not even be allowed at times. If you do not specify a time limit, the order will usually default to a day order.

Your broker may also have variations on GTC orders such as: good this week (GTW), good this month (GTM) and good through date (GTD) orders, which designate an order good through a specific date.

Instead of a day or GTC order, you can, instead, elect your time-frame to be immediate-or-cancel or fill-or-kill also known as IOC and FOK orders respectively. Both orders are asking for an immediate execution or cancellation of the order. The difference is that immediate-or-cancel orders allow for partial fills while fill-or-kill orders must be filled in their entirety.

Orders That Control Execution Size: All-or-None, Minimum Lots

If you place a limit order, for example, to buy 30 contracts at a limit of $5, it is possible to get filled on only a portion, say 20 contracts. With a limit order, you are telling your broker to buy *up to* the amount designated (30 contracts in this example).

All-or-None

If, however, you want to ensure that you get all 30 contracts or nothing at all, you need to use an "all-or-none" restriction (AON). If you use this restriction, you are telling the floor to fill the entire order, or nothing at all.

There is a big danger in using all-or-none orders, though. Any order marked all-or-none goes to the back of the line (for listed stocks), or is held in the back pocket of an options or futures trader. This means that it is possible you'll never get an execution, even though many traded at your price or better, and you cannot hold the exchange to time and sales. The trader can always come back and say that all contracts could never be filled at once and you will have no recourse against your broker or the exchange. Additionally, quotes to fill AON orders do not need to be within the current bid-ask range.

Minimums and Minimum Lots

If you don't like the idea of all-or-none restrictions, you can opt for a minimum. For example, say you are selling 50 contracts but you want at least 30 or nothing at all. You can place the order to sell 50 with a minimum of 30.

Additionally, if you only want your trade filled in minimums of five contracts thereafter, you can tell your broker "minimum lots" of five. So the order would look like "sell 50 contracts, minimum 30, and minimum lots five." Now the order must be filled with at least 30 initially and in lots of five thereafter such as 35, 40, etc., up to 50.

Minimums and minimum lots are nice alternatives to all-or-none orders.

Canceling Your Order: Straight Cancellation, One Cancels Other

If you have placed an order other than a market order and wish to cancel it, you can do so by simply placing a straight cancellation order. Remember that market orders are guaranteed to fill, which is why you cannot request a cancellation of a market order. The second it hits the floor it's filled.

Once the floor receives your cancellation request, they will check to see if your order may have already been filled. If not, they will honor the request and cancel the order. However, you must understand that a cancellation order is technically a "request" to cancel and does not guarantee a cancellation. Just because you do not see a confirmation on your account does not necessarily mean that the order has not been filled. In many cases, the execution could have taken place minutes ago but just took a while for the floor to get the confirmation back to the broker.

OCO Orders (One Cancels Other, or Order Cancels Order)

An OCO order is used to change orders so you don't risk getting two of them filled. Let's say you placed an order for the Microsoft futures contract at $60, the market is now rallying, and you do not have a confirmation back yet. If you decide to pay a higher price, you can call your broker and say to buy the contract at a higher price, say $60.50 OCO.

This means your order will be presented at the new price of $60.50 and, if filled, will automatically cancel the first order to buy at $60. If the order has already been filled at $60, the new order at $60.50 is cancelled.

Confirming Your Order

Your broker will be able to execute and confirm your order with the same ease and speed you're probably familiar with in the stock market. It will usually take a matter of seconds to confirm your market order.

Let's say you are filled at $61. This means you have agreed to buy 100 shares of Microsoft for a price of $61 per share at expiration of the futures contract. Again, this is a total contract value of $6,100, so you will be required to put up the initial margin amount of 20%, or $1,220. As a reminder, we'll assume the maintenance level is $976.

At the end of that day and every trading day thereafter, your account will be marked to market. It will be debited if the contract value falls and credited if it rises. Remember that futures contracts and stocks are traded on separate exchanges, so they do not necessarily move hand-in-hand. But as we learned in Chapter 4, arbitrage keeps the prices separated by roughly the cost of carry. The result is that your long position should rise (fall) when the underlying stock rises (falls). Assume that the Microsoft futures contract has the following settlement prices over the next 10 days:

62.30
59.60
59.15
58.25
59.62
60.88
58.75
61.09
62.30
64.05

Figure 6.3 shows how your account would look at the end of each trading day:

Long Futures Position at $61					
Day	Settlement price	Net change	Gain/ Loss	Account balance	Remarks
				Initial deposit (margin): +$1,220	Contract purchased. Deposit 20% of $6,100 contract value
1	62.30	+1.30	+130	$1,350	Equity increased by $130
2	59.60	-2.70	-270	$1,080	Equity decreased but still above maintenance margin of $976
3	59.15	-0.45	-45	$1,035	Equity decreased again but still above maintenance margin of $976
4	58.25	-0.90	-90	$945 = maintenance call	Equity falls below maintenance margin of $976. Send broker check (variation margin) for $275 to bring equity back to initial $1,220
5	59.62	+1.37	+137	$1,357	Equity increased
6	60.88	+1.26	+126	$1,483	Equity increased
7	58.75	-2.13	-213	$1,270	Equity decreased
8	61.09	+2.34	+234	$1,504	Equity increased
9	62.30	+1.21	+121	$1,625	Equity increased
10	64.05	+1.75	+175	$1,800	"Sell to close" futures contract for $64.05 — contract closed out

Figure 6.3

Notice how the price of the contract fluctuates from a low of $58.25 to a high of $64.05. In turn, your account equity is changed by that same change in value of the contract. For example, after the first day, the contract settles at $62.30, which is up $1.30. Because each contract represents 100 shares, your account is credited with $130 and your equity rises by that same amount. Notice too that it's okay if the account equity falls, as long as it does not fall below the maintenance level of $976, such as between days two and three. Once the maintenance level of $976 is broken, though, you must send a variation margin check to bring the account back up to the initial margin level of $1,220.

What's interesting to note is that although your account is debited and credited daily, the only thing that matters to your total equity is where the contract finishes. For example, say the contract settles up one additional dollar on day eight at $62.09 rather than $61.09 as shown. The means the net change would be $3.34 instead of $2.34. If so, would we have an additional $100 in the account and receive $1,900 rather than $1,800 at the end? No, because that additional gain will be exactly mirrored in the opposite direction on the following day. For instance, on day nine, the net change would only be up 0.21 instead of $1.21. That's because the contract would rise from $62.09 to $62.30 for a 21-cent gain. On day ten, the net change would still be the same $1.75 rise. The result is that day eight would increase by $1 and day nine would fall by $1 for no net change. *The only thing that matters to total equity is where the contract starts and where it finishes.*

This leads to an even quicker way to calculate gains and losses for futures. In the list of settlement prices in Figure 6.3, we know the contract was purchased for $61 and ended up at $64.05. This means a gain of $64.05 - $61 = $3.05 was realized for a total gain of $305. Additionally, a check for $275 was sent, so the total equity must be increased by $305 + $275 = $580. If we add $580 to the starting value of $1,220 we get $1,800, which is the same result obtained by going through all the debits and credits.

In order to find our gains or losses on a futures contract, we only need to know the opening price and the closing price. Notice that this is the same for stocks as well, so there really is no difference between buying the futures contract and buying the stock in terms of gains and losses due to price movements. An investor buying 100 shares of stock at $61 and selling for $64.05 would realize the same $305 gain. The difference between one trader buying futures and another buying stock is that the futures trader is debited and credited daily, whereas the stock trader only has "paper" gains or losses.

Using Figure 6.3 we can see that a trader buying stock for $61 would have an *unrealized loss* of $275 with the stock at $58.25 during day four. The futures trader must send a check for this amount, but the stock trader does not have to. The reason the stock trader doesn't need to send money is because the stock is paid for in full and cannot fall below zero. The futures trader, however, is leveraged by placing a "good faith" deposit (initial margin) of only $1,220 in anticipation of paying $6,100 at expiration. If the futures trader deposited the full contract value of $6,100 at the beginning, there would be no difference at expiration between the futures trader and the stock trader.[13]

The Short Position

Let's run through a short futures contract to be sure you understand how they work. To make it easy, we'll use the above example but look at it from the trader's perpective who is short the contract and matched with this long position.

To start, we know that futures are a zero-sum game, so if we do our calculations correctly we should find that the short contract ends up with a loss of $305, which is exactly the gain of the long position. Figure 6.4 summarizes the same transactions for the short position:

Short Futures Position at $61					
Day	Settlement price	Net change	Gain/ Loss	Account balance	Remarks
				Initial deposit (margin): +$1,220	Contract sold at $61. Deposit 20% of $6,100 contract value
1	62.30	+1.30	-130	$1,090	Equity decreased by $130 but still above maintenance margin of $976
2	59.60	-2.70	+270	$1,360	Equity increased
3	59.15	-0.45	+45	$1,405	Equity increased
4	58.25	-0.90	+90	$1,495	Equity increased
5	59.62	+1.37	+137	$1,358	Equity decreased
6	60.88	+1.26	-126	$1,232	Equity decreased
7	58.75	-2.13	+213	$1,445	Equity increased
8	61.09	+2.34	-234	$1,211	Equity decreased
9	62.30	+1.21	-121	$1,090	Equity decreased
10	64.05	+1.75	-175	$915	"Buy to close" futures contracts for $64.05 — contract closed out

Figure 6.4

The short trader must also post the initial margin requirement of $1,220. Shorting a futures contract is not like shorting stock, as the trader does not receive a credit. However, the short stock trader still has to post Reg T and pay 50% above the initial credit amount for security, whereas the futures trader only pays 20%. It is still far cheaper and easier to short futures than stock.

---

[13] Of course, dividends, voting privileges, or other rights conveyed with stock ownership will not carry over to the futures trader. However, we are talking about differences due solely to price movements in the stock.

Because the stock closes up $1.30 after the first day, the short trader is down by $130 for a position value of $1,090. There is no need to send a check because he is still above maintenance margin of $976. Days two through nine are straightforward; the trader gains when the stock falls and loses when it rises. After the tenth day, the account is down to $915, which would require variation margin to be sent in. However, because we assume it is closed out on this day, there is no need to send a check. This trader started with $1,220 equity and ended up with $915, which is a loss of $305 — exactly what we predicted. Once again we can take the shortcut method and realize that the contract was shorted at $61 and repurchased for $64.05, which is a loss of $3.05 or $305 when taking into account the 100-share size of the contract.

In Chapter 1, we said that futures trading can be risky, depending on how it is used. Now you should understand why. In this example, if you have the $6,100 and want to invest in Microsoft, there is really no difference whether you buy the stock or the futures. With the futures though, you get access to your gains immediately without having to close the position. This is something the stock trader cannot do.

However, if you do not have the money and wish to *speculate* in the futures market, you can do so by placing a small amount down, such as the $1,220 in the example. But if you trade futures in this manner, great damage can be done. If you start receiving maintenance calls from your broker and don't have the money, they may close out your contract or even journal money from another account you may have with them. If they close out the contract for a loss, you are still responsible for that loss. These rights are given to them in the account agreement form you must sign in order to open the account. In this example, when the stock (futures) was $58.25 during day four, you may have been forced to close out the contract if you couldn't send a check immediately (you'll still be liable for the $275 though).

Notice that with the stock or futures at $64.05 that a gain would have resulted (for the long position) had you been allowed to hang on to the contract. This is the dangerous aspect of futures. Most of the commodity contract values are very large, and many people don't have the kind of money readily available to pay for one contract outright. Because of this, many are forced to close contracts early even though conditions may turn in their favor in the end. Keep this in mind when you start trading futures contracts. Use contract values that are manageable and that allow you to send in variation margin if that should happen. If you don't, one slight unexpected move can cause you to be out for a permanent loss. A better way to play the futures is to ask yourself if you can, or are comfortable, controlling a contract of that size rather than determining if you can afford the initial margin amount.

Questions

1) Which of the following orders guarantees the execution?

   a) limit
   b) market
   c) OCO

2) Which of the following orders guarantees the price?

   a) limit
   b) market
   c) OCO

3) What is the difference between a stop order and a stop limit order?

4) You purchased one single-stock futures contract two months ago at $30 and it settled today at $41. What are your total gains? Do you need to know all of the net changes up to today in order to calculate your gains?

5) You purchased a futures contract with an initial margin requirement of $2,000 and maintenance margin of $1,600. The underlying stock closed down again today, leaving your account value at $1,500. Do you need to send in variation margin? If so, how much?

6) You wish to buy a futures contract to participate in upward price movements. Your initial trade would be:

   a) buy to open
   b) sell to open
   c) buy to close
   d) sell to close

7) You wish to get out the contract you entered in Question #6. What do you do now?

   a) buy to open
   b) sell to open
   c) buy to close
   d) sell to close

8) You wish to sell a futures contract to profit from downward price movements. Your initial trade would be:

    a) buy to open
    b) sell to open
    c) buy to close
    d) sell to close

9) You wish to close out the contract you entered in Question #8. What do you do now?

    a) buy to open
    b) sell to open
    c) buy to close
    d) sell to close

Answers

1) Which of the following orders guarantees the execution?

    b) market

2) Which of the following orders guarantees the price?

    a) limit

3) What is the difference between a stop order and a stop limit order?

A stop order is guaranteed to fill if the stop price is traded at or through (below). It does not guarantee a price. For a stop limit order, two prices must be given to your broker — a stop price and a stop limit price. The order is activated if the stop price is traded at or through (below). However, the order will only be filled if the order can be filled at the stop limit price or better (more favorable).

4) You purchased one single-stock futures contract two months ago at $30 and it settled today at $41. Do you need to know all of the net changes up to today in order to calculate your gains? What are your total gains?

You do not need to know all of the gains or losses. The net effect is that the contract is effectively closed each day and rewritten.

This contract, at the end of the day, will leave this trader with a gain of $11 * 100 shares, or $1,100 gain in total.

5) You purchased a futures contract with an initial margin requirement of $2,000 and maintenance margin of $1,600. The underlying stock closed down again today, leaving your account value at $1,500. Do you need to send in variation margin? If so, how much?

Because your account fell below the maintenance margin level of $1,600, you must send in variation margin. This means you need to bring your account back up to the initial margin level, so you would have to send $500 to your broker.

6) You wish to buy a futures contract to participate in upward price movements. Your initial trade would be:

    a) buy to open

7) You wish to get out the contract you entered in Question #6. What do you do now?

    d) sell to close

8) You wish to sell a futures contract to profit from downward price movements. Your initial trade would be:

    b) sell to open

9) You wish to close out the contract you entered in Question #8. What do you do now?

    c) buy to close

Chapter 7
Strategies

We've covered a lot of ground on futures contracts and have shown you the basics of how they trade. It's now time to shift gears and look at the various ways we can use futures to help our investments. If you still don't think futures can play an important part in your portfolio, please read on, as we will cover many strategies from the conservative to the highly leveraged. There will almost certainly be a strategy for everyone.

Because futures contracts offer the same straight-line profit and loss profile as stock (Figure 3.1 in Chapter 3), most of the strategies used in stock trading can be transferred to futures. Futures just give an added edge in that they require far less money down to control the same number of shares and are usually easier to move in and out of.

Let's look at some basic strategies and then we'll cover some general strategies at the end.

Long Futures Position

One of the most basic uses of futures is for speculation. If you think a stock is going to move higher, you now have the choice of buying a futures contract instead of the stock. As we've shown, this revolutionary new asset can provide significant leverage. Let's say you think the Nasdaq will move higher over the next three months.

The Nasdaq 100 (NDX) is a cash-settled index, which means they only settle in cash. You cannot take delivery of the 100 stocks in the index. Their contracts trade at the Chicago Mercantile Exchange (CME) and have a value of $100 times the level of the NDX. Currently the NDX is currently 1204, which means the total value of that contract is 1204 * $100 = $120,400, yet the initial margin is only $15,000 with maintenance margin set at $12,000. The $15,000 initial margin represents slightly more than 12% of the contract value.

The September contract is currently trading at 1216 with 140 days to expiration. By purchasing the contract, you are agreeing to pay the cash value of the index at a price of 1216 * $100 = $121,600. To do so though, you only need to put $15,000 down to control that contract.

Let's assume you are correct and the NDX rallies to a level of 1300, which is up 96 points. At that point, the futures contract can be sold for at least 1300 for a profit of (1300 - 1216) * $100 = $8,400. We say the contract can be sold for "at least" 1300 because there will likely be some cost of carry associated with it just as when we purchased the contract for 1216 even though the index was trading for 1204.

Ready to see some real leverage at work? Figure 7.1 shows the Nasdaq 100 Index between October 1999 and May 2002. Between October 1999 and late March 2000 (shown between the first two vertical bars in Figure 7.1), the Nasdaq 100 climbed from 2334 to 4816, representing more than a 100% increase in less than 160 days. While this may sound rare, it can and does happen with volatile indices more often than you may think.

If you had purchased the contract for about 2340 (2334 plus some cost of carry) and sold for 4816, that would net a profit of (4808 - 2334) * $100 = $247,600 for $15,000 down and virtually no maintenance calls along the way. Of course, it would be unlikely that you catch the index at the start of a great run and sell it at the peak; however, this example shows that aggressive movements occur in the markets and a lot of money can be made for very little invested. Even if you only caught a fraction of that move you could have easily doubled your money in virtually no time at all.

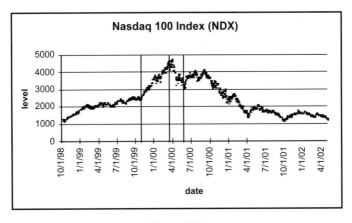

Figure 7.1

E-Mini Nasdaq 100 Contracts

Incidentally, there are a series of "e-mini" contracts traded at the CME. The "e" stands for "electronic" and the "mini" represents the fact that they are reduced in size. The e-mini Nasdaq contracts are one-fifth the size of the regular contract, which means their multiplier and initial margin requirements are reduced by one-fifth. Rather than posting $15,000 for a regular Nasdaq 100 contract, as in the previous example, only $3,000 is required to take a position in the e-mini contracts. Of course, for a given move in the Nasdaq 100, your profit (or loss) on the e-mini's will only be one-fifth as large as compared to the regular contracts as they have a multiplier of $20 instead of $100. The e-mini contracts trade virtually 24 hours throughout the day, so you can participate in market moving events before the stock market even opens for business. There are even e-mini versions of the S&P 500, S&P 400, Russell 2000 and others. You can read more about these contracts by going to the following link on the Internet: www.cmc.com/products/indcx/indcx.cfm

How many other assets allow you instant access to a basket of 100 stocks or more and allow point-for-point profit and loss (unlike most options) for only $3,000 down? There aren't any. In fact, most mutual funds require an investment of at least $2,500 to even buy in to them but will only execute them at that evening's closing price. You will not be able to trade them during the day as you can with a futures contract. Additionally, many mutual funds have minimum required holding periods and will not let you even trade out of it the next day without a penalty of some kind. There are just some things that can't be done using anything but a futures contract.

Creating Your Own Index

Another great feature about futures contracts is that they allow us to custom tailor indices for a very low cost. What if you liked the Nasdaq 100 but didn't like one of the stocks in it? That's easy to fix with futures. You can simply buy the NDX contract and short the contract of the company you do not like, in proper proportions, which effectively spins that company out of the index and creates your very own Nasdaq 99. The possibilities are endless, and there is no other vehicle that allows it to be done so easily and efficiently as a futures contract.

Short Futures Position

Opposite the long futures position is the short futures position. If you think a stock or index is going to fall, you can simply sell a futures contract as your opening trade and you will profit if you are correct. Remember, there is no need for an uptick and no 50% Reg T requirement. You simply post your initial margin requirement as the long position does, and you are short the contract. As with the previous long position example, this would require a $15,000 initial margin deposit. Looking back to Figure 7.1, the NDX fell from 4816 in late March 2000 to 2897 in late May 2000. This 61-day period is shown between the second two vertical bars in that chart. A short contract at 4816 and a purchase at 2897 would yield (4816 - 2897) * $100 = 191,900 with virtually no maintenance calls during this short 61-day period. Using the e-mini contracts would only require $3,000 initial margin and would yield over $38,000.

Additional Advantages of Short Futures over Short Stocks

We mentioned earlier that SSFs offer big advantages to speculators, as it will be easier to enter short positions because there is no uptick requirement and no need for your broker spend time calling his stock loan department. While the process of shorting stocks is usually quite fast, it can become time consuming if shares are hard to locate. If so, you may be put on a waiting list while your brokerage firm tries to locate shares at other firms, which is known as "shopping the street," to see if they have shares available to borrow. By the time they locate the shares, which is not even definite, the trading opportunity may have already passed.

This can be further complicated if the stock is "restricted," which is usually designated by an "R" next to the live quote (this used to be designated by the code "UPC 71" named after the rule). If a security is restricted, that means that it represents an aggregate clearing short position of 10,000 or more shares that is greater than or equal to one half of one percent of the total shares outstanding. In these cases, your broker will likely have a tough time finding those shares and will charge you a higher corresponding margin requirement.

There is a hidden danger in short stock positions, mainly in restricted shares, that many traders do not know about. It is possible, although unlikely, that you could be forced to close a short stock position if the long position wishes to sell his shares and the broker-age firm cannot find another short position to take your place.[14] This will not happen with a futures contract, as there are no limits to the amount of open interest that can exist. The open interest solely depends on how many people wish to enter contracts to buy and sell the underlying stock in the future.

You may be thinking that, despite all the benefits of futures contracts, short stocks have a distinct advantage since there is no time limit on them. However, futures contracts can easily be rolled forward, thus keeping you in the short position until you decide to close it out. For example, say it is now January and you are short a March contract. Once March expiration nears, you can then buy March back and sell another distant month such as June. This process can continue indefinitely.

---

[14] Nasdaq UPC 11830 and NYSE Rule 282.

In addition to the speed, ease, and confidence that single-stock futures offer short sellers, there is yet another advantage. It will usually be much cheaper from a *net interest* standpoint to enter a short futures contract than to post the Reg T amount for a traditional short sale.

For example, say you wish to short 500 shares of Microsoft at $60. The total value of that position is 500 * $60 = $30,000, which means you must post 50% of that for Reg T, or $15,000 of your own money. However, if you sell five futures contracts at $60, you would only need to post 20%, or $6,000. The futures seller will earn the risk-free rate over time since the value of the futures contract must be today's spot price plus the cost of carry. The short stock trader will pay interest on the $30,000 loan but earn interest on the $45,000 in proceeds. Depending on those rates, the futures contract will usually come out the clear winner in terms of net interest charges.

The net interest advantage is often cited as one of the reasons for the holdup of the introduction of single-stock futures. Because it is faster and more efficient to short futures than stocks, brokerage firms are afraid of losing significant interest income from the lending of securities. Powerful lobbyists are sure to be at work to prevent this economic benefit from being passed to the investor.

Once again, futures offer all of the advantages with none of the disadvantages in using stocks. Hopefully you are starting to see why it will be so important to understand these tools before they debut.

Covered Calls

Covered call writing is a strategy where the investor buys the underlying stock and then sells a call against that stock. For example, if you buy 100 shares of Intel at $28 and then sell a $30 Intel call, that is a covered call position. Which strike price to use is a matter of preference. If the investor writes a $30 call, there will be more premium than if a higher strike, such as a $35, is written. The higher premium allows for more downside protection while the higher strikes allow for more potential gains in the stock. The reason the strategy is considered "covered" is because the investor will always be able to deliver the shares if the long call owner decides to exercise their right and demand the stock. In other words, the risk of higher and higher stock prices is eliminated — the investor already owns the shares.

This is not to say that the covered call strategy is without risk. The risk, however, is to the downside since the covered call investor owns the stock. If the stock falls substantially, the investor will lose that value but can only gain a fixed amount from the sale of the call. Once that premium is depleted, the strategy heads into losing territory.

For example, let's assume an investor buys Intel stock at $28 and sells a two-month $30 call for $1.25. If so, the investor's cash outlay is reduced by the amount of the premium, which gives a new cost basis of $28 - $1.25 = $26.75. There are three important rates of return to compare. First, if the stock is exactly the same price at expiration, the investor profits by the $1.25 premium and the gain is $1.25/$26.75 = 4.7%. Another method is to realize that the investor paid $26.75 for a stock now worth $28, which is a 4.7% increase. Regardless of which method you use, it is important to annualize that rate since it was earned after only two months rather than one year. Because there are 12/2 = 6 groups of two-month periods in a year, we need to multiply the 4.7% return by 6 for an annualized rate of about 28%. This is called the "static" rate of return since it assumes the stock has not moved.

Another rate we want to look at is the "return if called" rate. As the name implies, this is the rate if the stock is called away (the investor is assigned). If the investor is assigned, they must give up the stock and receive the strike price of $30 in exchange. If this happens, the covered call writer nets a gain of $3.25 (buys at $26.75 and sells for $30) for a rate of 12.15%, or nearly 73% on an annualized basis.

As stated earlier, the risk of the covered call is that the underlying stock falls. If the stock falls, the investor may lose money, but he will not lose as much as another investor who just holds the stock. This is because the $1.25 premium provides some cushion to hedge the long stock position. So a third rate we need to look at is the "breakeven" rate, which is simply the percent fall the stock can sustain and the investor breaks even. In this example, we are assuming the investor paid $28 for the stock, which means it can fall to a level of $28 - $1.25 = $26.75, which is about a 4.5% fall. We do not need to annualize this rate, as we're only concerned with the actual percentage drop we can sustain and still break even. If the stock falls 4.5%, we just break even on our investment. Notice how a stockowner at $28 would be down 4.5% had the call not been written. This shows that covered calls provide some downside protection.

Depending on which month and strike you choose, all of the above rates of return will change. If you find a set that suits your particular needs, that is the month and strike you want to write. Higher strike calls will bring in less money but provide a higher "return if called" rate, while lower strike calls will bring in more money and provide a higher "breakeven" rate.

Using this covered call analysis for stocks, we can carry it over to futures. Once again, the only difference you will find is that the leverage will be about five times greater due to the low 20% initial margin rates on single-stock futures.

For example, let's assume this investor instead buys a single-stock futures contract on Intel at $28 and then sells the $30 call. The total contract value is $2,800 and the initial margin requirement, assuming 20%, will be $560. The futures buyer is required to put $560 down but receives $125 from the sale of the call for a net deposit of $435. To find the static returns, we assume the futures contract can be sold for $28, which is the same as the purchase price, so it nets no gain or loss to the buyer. The futures buyer effectively invests $435 and collects $560 at expiration for a net gain of about 28.7%, or 172% annualized. With $125 credit from the call option sitting in the account, the single-stock futures position can drop to a level of $435 before breaking even.

There are some important points to consider with covered calls on futures. First, remember that the above calculations are assuming all else constant. In the real world, we are exposed to basis risk, so the above calculations will sometimes be improved and sometimes won't. Second, we are assuming the sale of an equity option — an option on stock — and not on futures. This is perfectly okay to do and may be more advantageous for you in some circumstances. Just be aware that you should probably sell the option contract that expires at the same time as the futures contract. That way, if you are assigned on the call and the stock is way up, you simply take delivery of stock from your futures contract. There is also the risk you could get assigned early on the calls, although this usually does not happen, as it's not in the call owner's best interest. However, if you are assigned on the call option early you cannot take delivery from your futures contract early. But you could always short sell the stock to make delivery and use the futures as a hedge.

There are many combinations of covered calls from which to choose. Now with single-stock futures — and eventually options on them — you will be able to utilize them more efficiently and with greater leverage.

Spreads

Simply defined, spreads are strategies that involve the buying of one contract and the selling of another one. The term "spread" is used since the trader attempts to profit from a change in the spread — the price difference between the two contracts — as opposed to an overall rise or fall in the underlying. For example, if a January Microsoft contract is $60 and a March contract is $60.75 then the spread is 75 cents to the March side. Let's assume that you buy the January contract and sell the March. If the price of the January contract rises faster than the March contract, you will make money. This is because the amount you make on your long position is greater than the amount you lose on the short position.

To see why, assume that the January contract rises to $61 and the March contract rises to $61.50. Notice that the spread has shrunk from 75 cents to 50 cents, which is a gain of 25 cents. We can also find this 25-cent profit by considering the individual contracts rather than the spread. The January contract rose $1 (from $60 to $61) while March only rose 75 cents (from $60.75 to $61.50). Therefore, you gained $1 on the long position and lost 75 cents on the short for an overall gain of 25 cents, which is exactly the same answer we got by just looking at the difference in the spreads between the opening and closing trades (see Figure 7.2).

Long January	Short March	Spread
$60	$60.75	75 cents
$61	$61.50	50 cents
Gain of $1	Loss of 75 cents	
Net gain of 25 cents		**Net gain of 25 cents**

Figure 7.2

Prices do not necessarily need to rise in order for the above trader to make money. For instance, it is possible for the January contract to fall from $60 to $59.70 while the March contract falls from $60.75 to $60.25. If so, the trader loses 30 cents on the long contract but gains 50 cents on the short contract for a net gain of 20 cents. A profit was made here because the short position fell by a larger amount than the long position. Figure 7.3 shows how the same trader can make money if prices fall:

Long January	Short March	Spread
$60	$60.75	75 cents
$59.70	$60.25	55 cents
Loss of 30 cents	Gain of 50 cents	
Net gain of 20 cents		**Net gain of 20 cents**

Figure 7.3

Please don't interpret this to mean that spreads will make money if prices rise or fall. We constructed both Figures 7.2 and 7.3 so that the trader either made more money on the long position than he lost on the short (7.2) or that he lost less money on the long position than gained on the short (7.3). Obviously there are other scenarios. If prices rise on both contracts as in Figure 7.2 but the short contract rises by a larger amount, then an overall loss will occur. Similarly, if prices fall as in Figure 7.3, we could have had the long position fall more than the short position, which would result in an overall loss as well.

Spreads on futures contracts are a little different from spreads with options. That's because options have strike prices and time premiums. With strike prices, there are arbitrage rules that definitively state which contract will be more valuable. For example, we know that a May $50 call will always be more valuable than a May $55 call. Similarly, we know a July $50 call will be more valuable than a May $50 call since there is more time remaining on the July option. Likewise, time premiums can determine whether the strategy is bullish or bearish. If a trader buys a May $50 call and sells a May $55 call, we know that it will result in a net debit, as the time premium on the $50 call will be higher than the $55. Because this spread is paid for (net debit) we know that money must be recouped in order for it to be profitable. So the strategy of buying a $50 call and selling a $55 call is bullish.

However, this is not so for futures. We may think a more distant contract should be more valuable, but there are no guarantees it must be so, as we learned in Chapter 5 with inverted markets. Also remember that futures contracts do not contain "time premium" above their cost of carry, so it will be impossible to tell if a futures spread trader is actually bullish or bearish just by looking at the position.

If you are using spreads on futures, you need to determine the pricing relationship between the two contracts; that is, which one will move higher or lower *relative* to the other?

Using spreads is a lower risk, lower reward strategy. In most cases, your broker will require smaller initial margin deposits if you are entering a spread order because of the reduced risk. Bear in mind that we say "in most cases." This is because your broker will want to see some type of correlation between the two assets. A high correlation simply means that the price movements are "tied together" by economic forces. Obviously buying a June Microsoft contract and selling a May Microsoft is highly correlated. If we see one Microsoft contract rise, we can be pretty sure that most of them have moved in the same direction.

Likewise, buying an airline contract and selling an oil contract is a highly correlated spread position. If oil prices rise, you can be pretty sure that airline prices will fall. Correlation does not mean that they must move in the same direction but only that we can be reasonably sure how they will move. In the case between airline stocks and oil stocks we would say the two are negatively correlated. So if you wish to enter a spread with no correlation such as purchasing a Microsoft contract and selling lean hogs, don't expect your broker to have a lower initial margin requirement!

The Mathematical Effects of Spreads

We said in Chapter 2 that diversification is a key factor in reducing the risk of any portfolio. Now we're going to look a little closer to find out why. The reason diversification helps is that the variability in any portfolio is largely caused by assets having positive correlation. In other words, when the stock market is up, most of the stocks in your portfolio will be up. When the market is down, most stocks will be down, too. Stocks tend to move in the same direction as other stocks. In order to reduce these tandem up and down swings, we need assets that pull in the opposite direction of each other — we need negative correlation.

Correlation is a statistical measure that shows the degree to which to variables move together. A "correlation coefficient" can be calculated and is between -1 and +1 inclusive. A correlation value of +1 means that the two assets are perfectly predictable. A move in one asset is matched by the other in exactly the same direction (because of the plus sign) and magnitude. Any stock therefore has a correlation of +1 with itself. A correlation coefficient of zero means there is no consistent way to predict the movement of one asset based on the other. In other words, the two assets move independently of each other; they are random. A correlation of -1 means the two assets are perfectly predictable but the minus sign tells us they move in the opposite direction. If one asset is up 2%, the other is down 2%.

If you are new to investing this may be a new concept for you, so we're going to demonstrate it with an example. Say you own a small engine manufacturing factory and produce nothing but lawn mowers. If so, your sales would be up in the spring and summer months when many people are buying lawn mowers. Conversely, sales would be down in the fall and winter months. Your business would be exposed to seasonal swings, which could hurt cash flows, profitability and growth. To guard against this, you could manufacture snowmobile engines, too. When lawn mower sales are high, snow mobile sales are low and vice versa — negative correlation — and the variability of your cash flows are smoothed out.

Any time we enter a spread order or add negatively correlated positions to our portfolio, we add a little bit of negative correlation to the portfolio and thereby eliminate some of the fluctuations, just as when snowmobile engines were added to the factory.

We can use negative correlation easily with futures contracts. We can buy a futures contract for one particular month and sell a different month, which is called an intramarket spread. We can even buy one contract of one company and sell another contract of a different company, which is called an intermarket spread. Regardless of which type is used, the sale of the second contract creates a negative correlation for the two positions because we're <u>selling</u> a positively correlated asset. The risk-reducing effects can be tremendous.

For example, you may hear of a strategy called "matched pair" trading, which is simply an intermarket spread. Using this strategy, the investor simultaneously buys and sells contracts of related companies such as IBM and Dell Computer. What does this accomplish? First, let's look at what happens to an investor who <u>purchases</u> both stocks. The effects of the purchase of these two related securities can be shown mathematically with the addition of a couple more statistical measures: *variance* and *covariance*.

The variance simply describes how much variability there is between prices. The exact meaning or calculation is not important for our purposes. Let's assume that the daily variance over the past year for IBM is 0.10% and 0.12% for Dell. If Dell and IBM were independent of each other (that is, no correlation) the total variance of these two positions would be 0.10 + 0.12 = 0.22. However, because they are in the same industry, they will tend to behave similarly. We can even test this with another statistical measure called the covariance, which is similar in concept to correlation and measures how strongly the two assets move together. Again, the formula or exact interpretation of it is not necessary to understand the benefits of spreads or diversification. Let's assume the covariance between these two stocks is 0.09% per day. Once we have this information, we can determine the total variance for the two stocks combined. It will be equal to the sum of the two variances plus an additional term, which is 2 * covariance between them. The total variance is therefore 0.10 + 0.12 + (2*0.09) = 0.40.

Notice how the variability has risen dramatically from 0.22 to 0.40 — nearly double — by purchasing both stocks. This is similar to waves moving across an ocean. If waves meet in any kind of synchronized way (positively correlated), they will get bigger. Only when they are moving opposite of each other (negative correlation) will they diminish in size. Positively correlated stocks combined in a portfolio only add to the variability; they don't reduce it.

While the investor who buys both stocks may have put his money in two separate stocks, there is very little diversification benefit here since both companies are highly correlated and will tend to rise and fall together. Figuratively speaking, the investor has put his eggs in separate baskets but has loaded those baskets onto the same truck (the computer industry). One of the biggest myths in the investment world is that the idea behind diversification is to buy different stocks across the same industry. The real objective is to not only have different stocks but, specifically, different stocks that are negatively correlated.

Let's see what happens with a matched pair trade and assume an investor buys IBM and sells Dell. If so, the formula is now changed and we must *subtract* the covariance between the two. The new variance for this investor in IBM would be 0.10 + 0.12 - (2*0.09) = .04% which is less than half the amount of original variability.

The ability to create short positions, whether for a spread or just to add to a portfolio, is one of the biggest advantages of single-stock futures for all investors. Even if you believe that shorting stocks or futures is too risky for you, it can be shown mathematically that the right contracts in the right amounts will actually reduce the variability of your portfolio — without reducing the returns. While this may sound counterintuitive, the concept is the foundation of modern portfolio theory, which gives a broad foundation for understanding market risk and reward.

There is no easier or more cash-efficient way to reduce the overall risk of your portfolio than with futures contracts.

General Strategies

The above strategies are basic yet specific strategies. At this point, we want to bring your attention to some general advantages of futures over stocks. There will be many ways to make use of these general descriptions and it is completely up to you to decide which strategy is best for you. While the following strategies are not specific, they are equally important as (if not more important than) the previous strategies, since they cause you to think about the various ways futures can be used to your benefit.

Diversification

In Chapter 2, we mentioned that a benefit of futures contracts is that they allow global diversification. Because of the low initial margin requirement, they can allow for safer investing through diversification on a domestic level, too. For instance, say you have $30,000 to invest in the stock market. If you buy quality companies, there's a good chance their share price will be high. Thus, you may not be able to afford many different stocks, which is key to diversification. Without going into the math, the bulk of company specific risk (called unsystematic risk) is washed away once you hold a properly balanced portfolio of about 16 to 22 stocks in different industries in your portfolio. In other words, if you own a little bit of tech, financials, automotive, healthcare, food and beverage, etc, you will end up with minimum risk for a given level of return, or conversely, a maximum return for a given level of risk. With only $30,000, however, you may not be able to obtain this optimal amount. But with single-stock futures, you have access to a tool that may be a key to smarter investing.

If you wish to buy a stock and hold it for a long time, such as five or 10 years, there's probably no doubt that purchasing the stock is your best bet. But what if you generally hold a stock for one year or so? Would you rather have two or three stocks or a basket of 20 one-year contracts? After all, we've shown there's no difference between the two positions in terms of price movement. You're better off with a larger basket, and futures contracts provide this opportunity.

Keep in mind that if you do this you may have to periodically send in money if a position goes against you. It may not be the best idea to invest *all* of your money so you still have some set aside to meet potential margin calls.

In addition, commodity futures are often highly uncorrelated with stocks. This simply means that there is no systematic association between commodities and stocks rising or falling together. The fact that many futures contracts are uncorrelated is a key to creating a properly diversified portfolio. We said earlier that unsystematic risk is nearly eliminated if you hold a properly balanced portfolio. Having low correlation between assets is what we mean by "properly balanced," and futures can be important for achieving this quality as demonstrated by the following facts:

- Stocks plunged 48% in 1973 and 1974 while the Goldman Sachs Agricultural Commodity Index rose 491%.

- Over the past 25 years, if you compare the major advances of the S&P 500 to futures, there were corresponding positive returns in futures as well. However, during all the largest S&P 500 stock declines, futures were positive. In all but one decline in the S&P 500, advances in futures completely offset losses in the S&P 500.

- Currently, the correlation between the S&P 500 and Barclay CTA Traders Index is .02 — virtually non-existent.[15]

Futures contracts can be your most effective source of portfolio balance. While nobody says you need to be 100% invested in futures, it is a mistake to completely ignore them.

Day-Trading

The diversification concept can be carried over to those who day-trade stocks. Day-traders are those who attempt to capture small

---

[15] The Barclay CTA Traders Index is a portfolio of professionally managed futures.

price movements, up or down, during the day and close all positions by the end of the day. Most day-traders pick a stock they are comfortable with and that they think will make a small move in a short time. Most of their expectations of these movements are based on technical analysis. Then they go for leverage by purchasing as many shares as they can with the money in their account. They hope to capture a sizeable profit on a small move many times throughout the day.

The problem with this approach is, once again, no diversification. The chances that a day-trader consistently picks a winning stock are slim to none. One or two losing trades quickly offset the winners. Futures contracts offer the leverage and diversification that day-traders seek. In fact, we can even carry it one step further and buy the stocks we think will rise and short the ones we think will fall. Yes, this can also be done with stocks, but it is far more expensive to meet the Reg T requirements. The end result is that you cannot get the same diversification with stocks as you can with futures, so you will therefore not have the same performance.

In fact, on February 27, 2001, the Securities and Exchange Commission (SEC) approved amendments to NASD Rule 2520. These amendments make some significant changes to the margin requirements for those who day-trade stocks. First, if you buy and sell a stock on the same day in a margin account and you do so at least four times in a rolling five-day business period, *you will be required to have a minimum equity balance of $25,000 before any more day trades can be placed.* On the good side, your "buying power" will be increased to a maximum of four times your excess margin. Regardless of this benefit, if you wish to actively day-trade stocks and do not keep a minimum balance of $25,000, then using single-stock futures will be your only way to continue day trading.

There is another benefit in futures trading for day-traders. As we've stated many times before, there's no need for an uptick, so there is no need to enter a "sell short" order. This makes it especially convenient if you wish to change directions during the day, which day-traders often do. In fact, they live for the daily price swings and try to capture upward as well as downward moves. Say you are long 300 shares of stock and you feel it is near an intraday high and wish to go short. To do so you must enter two separate orders. The first order is to sell 300 shares and the second order is to "sell short" 300 shares. Once again, it is necessary to separate the two orders due to the uptick rule. Now assume you are long 300 futures contracts instead and wish to go short 300 contracts. You simply enter one order to sell 600 contracts and you are now short 300. Notice how it takes just one quick futures trade to completely reverse your direction, whereas it takes two separate trades to do so with stocks.

Besides lower requirements, day-traders get the advantage of switching directions with precise responses to the market. If you are day-trading, using futures will be like maneuvering through the markets in a high-performance sports car. There will be no other vehicle more perfect for you than a single-stock futures contract.

Fine-Tuning and Rebalancing Your Portfolio

Futures are perfect for fine-tuning your existing positions. Say you have a long position that has fallen significantly but you are still bullish on it. You wish to purchase more shares to reduce your cost basis, which will allow you to reach breakeven sooner. Rather than spending a lot of money (and possibly being wrong) you can throw a relatively small amount toward a futures contract and gain the additional exposure without using all of your capital.

You can also use them to fine-tune your portfolio. Say you have a large blue-chip portfolio but you think a couple of other sectors that you don't own are about to make a run. For just a little bit of money, you now have exposure to those sectors and can enhance your returns if you are correct, without the need for a lot of money to do so.

Hedging 401(k) Accounts

You may have a 401(k) or other tax-advantaged account that does not allow sales except within certain time periods. If a stock in that account has made a nice run, you may not be able to do anything about it if you're in a restricted time period. However, with futures contracts, you can short the contract covering the same stock in another account; that will offer you a hedge, basically locking in a selling price. For example, say your company stock has run from $30 to $70 but you're not allowed to make a sale. Instead, you can sell one futures contract in another account for every hundred shares of stock you own. If the stock continues to rise, the gain in the shares will offset the losses on the futures. If the stock falls, the gain in the futures contracts will offset the losses in the 401(k).

Keep in mind this is one case where shorting stocks may not even work for you, since most companies do not allow employees to short company stock. Futures may be your only tool.

Please remember about marking to market though. If you short the futures contract and the stock continues to rise, you may get maintenance calls from your broker and you'll need to meet those. Even though you are effectively hedged with the long positions in the 401(k), you cannot access those funds until you sell those shares! So if you use futures in one account to hedge another account that you can't immediately access, make sure you have additional funds to meet potential maintenance calls.

Using Narrow-Based Indices

One of the more powerful products that will come about with SSFs is that of narrow-based indices. We learned in Chapter 3 that the Shad-Johnson Accord stalled futures trading on individual stocks as well as narrow based indices.

Now that the ban is lifted, you will see many indices designed to reflect smaller sectors, rather than the broad based indices such as the S&P 500 or the Nasdaq 100. In fact, OneChicago Exchange is planning to have indices on the following sectors:

- **Energy:** Natural gas, utilities, transmission, extraction services, high technology companies

- **Personal Computer Makers:** Computer storage, database software, security, online markets

- **Health Care Providers:** HMOs, pharmaceuticals, hospital operators

- **Telecommunications:** Wireless, networking, infrastructure

There will no doubt be additions to the list as the popularity of these indices increases. How can this help you? Say you are bullish on the computer sector. Rather than trying to pick the one or two manufacturers that will perform the best, you can simply pay one commission and buy a basket of stocks in that industry. In a sense, these will act like mini leveraged mutual funds.

Relative Strength Investing

This is a great strategy if you are banking on one company doing better than one of its competitors. Simply buy the futures contract of the company you like and short the contract of the competitor. As long as your prediction is correct, you stand to make gains. For instance, even if both companies rise, as long as your favorite rises more (does better) you have a bigger gain in the long futures position than you do a loss in the short contract, which nets you a gain. If both companies fall but your favorite doesn't fall as much (again, it performs better on a relative scale), then your short contract will provide more gains than the losses on the long contract. If your favorite rises and the competitor falls, then that's a double win since you make money on the long and short contracts.

However, if the competitor performs better on a relative scale, then an overall loss will occur. Keep in mind this is not a flaw in the strategy. In the first three cases we presented, your favorite company (the long position) performed better on a relative scale, and this was the prediction. However, in order to create an overall loss, your prediction must turn out to be wrong and the competitor (short position) must perform better on a relative scale. As long as your prediction holds true and the long position performs better than the short position on a relative scale, an overall gain at expiration results. Remember, we can't be sure that a gain will result *prior* to expiration because of basis risk.

Most of the strategies you've used or read about with equities can be interchanged with futures. Futures just provide a more cash-efficient means of utilizing them.

Questions

1) You are bearish on gold. Do you buy or sell the futures contract as an opening transaction?

2) Which of the following is a covered call?

 a) buy futures and sell futures
 b) buy futures and sell put
 c) sell futures and buy put
 d) buy futures and sell call

3) Which of the following is a spread?

 a) buy futures and sell futures
 b) buy futures and sell put
 c) sell futures and buy put
 d) buy futures and sell call

4) What is one advantage of using spreads?

 a) lower risk
 b) lower initial margin
 c) higher return

5) Would you expect K-Mart and Wal-Mart to be positively or negatively correlated?

6) If you are building a well-diversified portfolio would you look for stocks with positive or negative correlation?

Answers

1) You are bearish on gold. Do you buy or sell the futures contract as an opening transaction?

You want short positions if you are bearish. You would enter a short futures contract on gold in hopes of repurchasing it for a lower price at a later date.

2) Which of the following is a covered call?

 d) buy futures and sell call

3) Which of the following is a spread?

a) buy futures and sell futures

4) What is one advantage of using spreads?

a) lower risk

Note: The lower initial margin (answer b) would be true for options since you are bringing in money from the short sale. However, you do not receive credit balances with futures contracts and must pay an initial margin requirement for both positions.

5) Would you expect K-Mart and Wal-Mart to be positively or negatively correlated?

These two stocks are virtually identical in their operations. You would expect them to be positively correlated — if one goes up you would expect the other to move up as well.

6) If you were building a well-diversified portfolio would you look for stocks with positive or negative correlation?

You want negative correlation to smooth out the company-specific fluctuations. Once those are removed, you will get a higher return for a given level of risk or, conversely, an equal return for lower risk. Adding negatively correlated assets is the key to good diversification.

Chapter 8
Options on Futures

If you have traded any derivatives up to now, chances are they were options on a stock or index. We have shown that futures contracts derive their value from price moves (or expected moves) in the underlying stock and are therefore derivatives. Well, it is expected that <u>two years after</u> single-stock futures begin trading, you will be able to buy options on additions futures, which is a derivative on a derivative! Although it's unclear at this time as to why there is a two-year waiting period, it is probably due to regulators wanting to see the single-stock futures market get established and any bugs worked out of the computer systems before trading derivatives on them. Futures options are currently traded on most commodities.

This book is not intended to focus on options, but we will cover some basics for those who may not be familiar with them. In addition, the next chapter covers a very important futures hedging strategy that involves options, so you will need to understand the basic terminology and mechanics. For an in-depth book on options and strategies, you may wish to reference *An Investors Guide to Understanding and Mastering Options Trading*, which is published by 21st Century Investor Publishing, Inc.

What Is an Option?

Options are simply legal contracts between two people giving the buyer of the option the right, *but not the obligation*, to buy or sell stock for a fixed price over a given time period.

Notice the distinction between this definition and our definition of a futures contract. The futures trader has the obligation to either buy or sell the underlying asset (assuming he does not enter an offsetting position) while the options trader has the right to either buy or sell without the obligation.

There are two types of options: **calls** and **puts**.

These contracts are standardized, meaning they control a fixed amount of shares and expire at the same time. Because of this standardization, they are traded on an exchange, just like shares of stock or futures contracts. The option contracts are usually highly liquid, which means there are many buyers and sellers standing by who are willing to buy or sell. You can buy an option contract with the same speed it takes you to call your broker and buy stock.

Long Call Options

A call option gives the owner the right, but not the obligation, to buy stock ("call" it away from the owner) at a specified price over a given time period.

In trading lingo, any asset that you buy is called a long position. If you buy a call option, you are the owner, and are long the contract. Notice that the owner, the long position, has the right, *but not the obligation*, to buy the underlying stock. You are allowed to purchase the stock for a fixed price, but are not required to do so. In other words, you have the *option* to buy — which is where these financial assets get their name. It is up to the owner of the call option to determine if that right should be used. Consequently, the most the call option owner can lose is the amount paid for the option.

The price at which you can buy the stock is called the *strike* price, which is kind of a slang term that got its use because that's where the deal — the contract — was *struck*. Generally, each contract controls 100 shares of stock, called the *underlying* stock.

Each contract is good only for a certain amount of time. Usually you can find options on futures with as little time as a couple of weeks and up to about one year. However, these are standardized time frames, so you don't get to pick the exact date you want it to expire.

Just as stock is traded in shares, options are traded in units called *contracts*.

If you buy one IBM March $100 call option (one contract), you have the right, but not the obligation to buy 100 shares of IBM (the underlying stock) for $100 per share (the strike price) through the expiration date in March, which is usually the third Friday of the month.[16]

Long Put Options

A put option allows the owner to *sell* their stock ("put" it back to someone else) for the strike price within a given time. As with call options, the put buyer (long position) has the right, but not the obligation. If you buy an IBM March $100 put, you have the right, but not the obligation, to sell 100 shares of IBM for $100 per share through the third Friday in March. As with call options, it is up to the put owner to determine if that right should be used and, consequently, the most the put option owner can lose is the amount paid for the option.

Buying a put option is similar to buying an auto insurance policy. You can buy a policy for a premium and collect the insurance value if you wreck your car. If you don't wreck your car, you are only out the amount of the premium. Likewise, you can buy a put option for a premium and turn it back to the insurer (the put seller) if your stock should crash (fall below the strike price). If the stock stays above the strike, you would let the "insurance" expire and lose only the premium you paid.

Short Calls and Puts

Notice that with either calls or puts, the buyers (the "long" positions) have the right, but not the obligation, to buy or sell. The investor on the other side (the seller of the option, also called the "short" position) has the obligation to fulfill the contract; he has no choice. If a long call owner decides to buy the stock, the short call trader must oblige and sell. Likewise, if long put owners decide to sell their stock, the short put traders must purchase the stock. *Regardless of whether*

---

[16] Technically, options expire on the Saturday following the third Friday of the expiration month. However, this is for clearing purposes and there is nothing the option trader can do with an option on Saturday. The third Friday of expiration month is the last trading day so, for practical purposes, it is the day you want to consider as expiration.

the short option seller is forced to buy or sell stock, the money received (called the premium) from the initial short trade is his to keep. That's his compensation for accepting the risk.

If you wish to actually purchase the underlying asset with a call option or to sell it by using a put option, you must submit *exercise* instructions to your broker. Usually your broker will charge the regular commission whether you to buy or sell the underlying asset in the open market or through an option exercise. Remember, it is only the long positions that can submit exercise instructions, as they are the ones who purchased that right. If a long position exercises, the short option position is said to be assigned on that option.

Equity and index options currently being traded are called *spot options* since they control the current, or spot, asset. For example, if you own an Intel call option and exercise it, you immediately own Intel stock. Options on futures, however, work a little differently. If you are long a futures call option, you have the right, but not the obligation, to buy the futures contract for a fixed price. If you exercise a futures call option, you will be long a futures contract, which means you cannot take delivery of the actual asset until expiration of the futures contract. If you are long a futures put option, you have the right, but not the obligation to sell (short) the futures contract at a fixed price.

Why trade options on futures? After all, it may seem unnecessary since you can already buy options on the actual asset. There are many reasons why someone would prefer an option on a future rather than the spot asset. For example, assume a jewelry manufacturer that makes graduation rings is about to enter the busy season. At this time he doesn't know how much gold he will need as orders have not yet been taken. If he waits for the orders, gold prices may rise, which may leave him with far less profit than expected and possibly with a loss. In order to hedge this risk, the manufacturer could enter into a long gold futures contract. But if gold falls, the manufacturer will incur a nearly a point-for-point loss. Now you may be thinking that we said throughout the text that this loss is offset by the manufacturer's ability to buy gold cheaper in the market. The fact that he "loses" on the futures contract is exactly offset by the lower prices in the spot market. However, that argument assumes that the hedger actually does, in fact, take delivery of the underlying asset. In this case, we are assuming that the manufacturer is not even certain that delivery will take place, so there is a big difference in assumptions and therefore a big difference in the type of hedge that should be in place.

Because the jewelry manufacturer is uncertain of the delivery, a futures option may be the perfect solution. For only a little money down, the manufacturer has locked in his price on the futures contract and limited his risk to the amount paid for the option. The act of guaranteeing a purchase price and limiting the downside risk is something that cannot be done through a straight purchase of a futures contract.

This example shows a conservative hedging use of options on futures. Of course, options will attract speculators who wish to place "bets" that the underlying market will move up or down. So why would a speculator buy options on futures rather than on the spot asset? One reason is liquidity. Many times the underlying asset, oddly enough, is not as liquid or as "price transparent" as the futures contract. For instance, if you wish to buy a treasury bond, your broker must make several phone calls to bond traders to obtain the best bid or offer, which is very time consuming. However, if you buy a treasury bond futures contract, you will have immediate price information and many willing buyers and sellers.

Another reason speculators like these options is because it is easier, if not just for the sake of being cheaper, to take delivery of the futures contract than of the underlying asset. For example, if you are long a call option and it's near expiration, you may need to take delivery of the underlying asset at that time, assuming that was your intent. Depending on the cost of the underlying asset, that can be a large cash outlay or require high borrowing costs if you use margin for stocks. However, if you are long a futures option, you will only need to take delivery of the futures contract, which only requires the nominal initial margin requirement.

Options on futures work in about the same way as options on equities. Most futures options are American-style, just as with equities, which means they can be exercised at any time prior to expiration.

Figure 8.1 gives a recap of the main differences between futures and options on futures:

Asset	Risk	Maximum gain	Margin?	Premium
Long or Short Futures	Unlimited	Unlimited	Yes	No
Long Option	Limited to premium paid	Unlimited	No	Yes
Short Option	Unlimited	Limited to premium received	Yes	No

Figure 8.1

Risk and Reward Comparisons: Stocks, Futures and Options

Let's compare four traders with four different assets. One buys 100 shares of $50 stock outright, another buys those same shares on margin, another buys the futures contract, and the last trader buys a futures call option. We will assume the underlying stock is $50. The option trader buys a $50 strike for a premium of $2, which is a total purchase price of $200 since each contract controls 100 shares. Figure 8.2 shows comparisons of the initial deposits, market exposure, max gain, and max loss:

	Stock Trader	Stock Trader on Margin	Futures Trader	Option Trader, $50 Strike
Initial Deposit	$5,000	$2,500	$1,500	$200
Market Exposure	$5,000	$5,000	$5,000	$5,000
Max Loss	$5,000	$5,000	$5,000	$200
Max Gain	Unlimited	Unlimited	Unlimited	Unlimited

Figure 8.2

Notice how all four traders have the same exposure to $5,000 worth of stock and they all have the potential for unlimited gains as long as the underlying stock keeps rising. The maximum loss, however, is far less for the option trader. He is only exposed to a $200 loss, which is the amount paid for the option. But do not forget that this limited downside luxury comes at a cost. If the stock is $50 at expiration, the option trader loses 100% of the investment while the other three do not. The stock trader only misses out on interest that could have been earned had the stock not been purchased. The margin stock trader will pay some margin interest and the futures trader will lose the cost-of-carry on the futures contract. Regardless, these are negligible losses compared to the option trader who loses everything if the stock is the same price at expiration.

Figure 8.3 shows a detailed look at the four traders under different stock prices.

The margin trader is also down $2,000 but, on a percentage basis, is down 80% because of the 2:1 leverage created by only placing 50% of the total cost down on the margin trade.

The futures trader only placed $1,000 down initially (see Figure 8.2) but would have an account value of -$1,000 if the stock fell to $30 at expiration according to Figure 8.3. He would have to send a check for $1,000 to bring his account to a zero balance and would thus lose the initial deposit plus the second one, or 200%. We could also determine this by looking at the 40% loss of the stock trader and realize that the futures trader has 5:1 leverage because of the 20% initial margin and 5 * 40% = 200%.

Stock Price	Stock Trader	% Gain/Loss	Margin Stock Trader	% Gain/Loss	Futures Trader	% Gain/Loss	Option Trader	% Gain/Loss
30	-2000	-40%	-2000	-80%	-2000	-200%	-200	-100%
35	-1500	-30%	-1500	-60%	-1500	-150%	-200	-100%
40	-1000	-20%	-1000	-40%	-1000	-100%	-200	-100%
45	-500	-10%	-500	-20%	-500	-50%	-200	-100%
50	0	0%	0	0%	0	0%	-200	-100%
55	500	10%	500	20%	500	50%	300	150%
60	1000	20%	1000	40%	1000	100%	800	400%
65	1500	30%	1500	60%	1500	150%	1300	650%
70	2000	40%	2000	80%	2000	200%	1800	900%

Figure 8.3

The option trader loses 100% for any stock price below $50 at expiration, whereas the other three traders do not necessarily. Also notice that if the stock closes at $50, the first three traders lose nothing but the option trader loses 100%. This clearly shows that all assets listed offer different sets of risks and rewards and should not be thought of as substitutes for one another.

Questions

1) What is the difference between a call option and a put option?

   a) A call is the right but not the obligation to buy the underlying asset. A put is the right but not the obligation to sell the underlying asset.

   b) A call is the right but not the obligation to sell the underlying asset. A put is the right but not the obligation to buy the underlying asset.

   c) A call is the obligation to buy the underlying asset. A put is the obligation to sell the underlying asset.

2) If you exercise a call option on single-stock futures, will you get the stock?

3) What are the differences between futures and options on futures?

4) It is the (long/short) option position who has the right to exercise that option.

5) If you exercise a call option, the other person is:

   a) exercised
   b) not notified
   c) assigned

Answers

1) What is the difference between a call option and a put option?

   a) A call is the right, but not the obligation to buy the underlying asset. A put is the right, but not the obligation to sell the underlying asset.

2) If you exercise a call option on single-stock futures, will you get the stock?

No, you would receive the futures contract. Of course, you could buy the stock with the futures contract at expiration but the futures call option gives you the right to buy the futures contract, not the stock.

3) What are the differences between futures and options on futures?

Futures are an agreement today to buy or sell the underlying asset in the future. Options, however, give the owner the right, but not the obligation, to buy the underlying futures contract. Another major difference is that there is no time premium (aside from the cost of carry) on futures, whereas volatility plays a major role in the pricing of options.

4) It is the (long/short) option position who has the right to exercise that option.

The long position decides if exercising the contract is optimal. The short position has the obligation to fulfill that request.

5) If you exercise a call option, the other person is:

c) assigned

Chapter 9
Exiting a Futures Contract Through the Options Market

In Chapter 1 we learned that single-stock futures would <u>not</u> be bound by daily price limits. Remember, on most commodities, the futures price is allowed to fluctuate only so much in a given day. This is done mainly to protect people from accruing unmanageable losses, and this daily accrual of gains and losses adds to the stability of the futures markets.

In many cases, if the underlying stock or futures contract is halted (temporarily stops trading) then so is trading in options. In other words, the options are not allowed to trade unless the underlying asset is trading.

However, there many futures contracts, especially commodities, where this is not the case. For example, the live cattle futures contract on the CME cannot trade at a price of more than $.015 per pound above or below the previous day's settlement price. If this futures contract settles at 80 cents per pound today, it cannot trade above 81.50 or below 78.50 tomorrow. While this may not seem like a large price fluctuation, keep in mind that the contract is for 40,000 pounds of cattle so a $.015 move is equal to 40,000 * .015 = $600 in either direction. But if those boundaries are broken and the commodity is locked limit for the day, the options on that commodity will continue to trade.

Some contracts, such as foreign currencies, generally do not have daily price limits. You cannot get locked out of a contract of this type since it is always allowed to trade regardless of price. Of course, the downside to this feature is that you may have to sustain a large loss to do so.

Then there are some contracts that are mixed and will have no price limit in the spot month (current month) but will have price limits for subsequent months. In addition, the price limits can sometimes be altered during the contract's life, which is called an *expandable price limit.* For example, the Lumber 110 futures contract[17] on the CME has the following rule for price limits:

Daily Price Limits for Lumber 110 Contract:
There shall be no price limit in the spot month.

There shall be a daily price limit of $10.00 per thousand board feet above or below the previous day's settlement price.

If the contract nearest to expiration that is subject to a daily limit settles on the limit bid for two successive days or on the limit offer for two successive days, then the price limit shall be raised to $15.00 per thousand board feet for all contracts subject to a daily limit.

If the contract nearest to expiration that is subject to a daily price limit of $15.00 does not settle at a limit bid or limit offer, without regard to market direction, the price limits shall revert to $10.00 per thousand board feet on the next business day.

Regardless of what type of futures contracts you may end up trading, it is crucial to understand how to exit one through the options market in the event the futures are locked limit but the options are still trading. Just because the SSFs will not have daily price limits doesn't mean you don't need to understand how to enter or exit a futures position through the options market. You may trade into a commodity at some time that does impose price limits and find yourself in a situation where this technique can save your portfolio. Additionally, each futures contract has a different set of rules regarding limit moves so it is certainly possible that a particular volatile stock may have trading limits imposed on it, even if only on a temporary basis, once options on SSFs begin trading.

This is invaluable information to understand if you are trading futures contracts. If a situation should arise where you need to enter or exit a futures contract through the options market, you will need

---

[17]This is called the Lumber 110 contract since it controls 110,000 board feet of random length 2x4s.

to understand how to do it *before* that time. Having your broker explain the strategy (assuming they can) during a distressful time will only lead to rushed, uninformed, and potentially disastrous decisions.

Example:

Let's assume you are short the live cattle futures contract at 78. Because you are short the contract, you will incur losses as the underlying rises. You may, for example, set a "mental stop" limit of 80. That just means that you are going to exit the contract by purchasing the same contract if it were to trade at 80 or higher.

Let's say a government report comes out, which is usually what drives commodity prices, that is favorable to this market (remember the movie *Trading Places*). Order flow indicates that the value of the contract should be 83 cents, but the market cannot exceed 81.50. Trading therefore would open up lock limit at 81.50, and no trades for that day could occur above this price. So while you may have planned to buy the contract back at 80, if it's limit up, you may find that you *cannot* buy it back. What's worse, it may trade limit up for days, leaving you in a potentially dangerous situation.

While trades are allowed to occur at or below that price, there is often a lack of sellers since the long positions are hoping for another increase the following day. Speculators, of course, are not willing to short the contracts, at least in great numbers, since everyone is expecting another increase for the following day. The result is that there just aren't that many sellers, and liquidity can be a real problem.

While new information can resume trading below this lock limit range in a hurry, what can you do in those times where it doesn't? Must you be forced to stay in your futures contract, possibly day after day, only to watch it continue trading against you?

Unfortunately, that is the only thing you can do — *unless you know how to hedge against this risk in the options market*. In order to understand this strategy, we need to understand synthetic options. While the name may sound intimidating, synthetic options are actually quite easy.

What Is a Synthetic Option?

A synthetic option is a combination of stock, calls, or puts that behave exactly like another set of stocks, calls, or puts from a profit and loss standpoint at expiration of the option. Specifically, of the three assets — stocks, calls, and puts — a particular combination of any two will produce the third. For example, long stock plus a long put is the same thing (synthetically equal) as a long call. We can show why by looking at a profit and loss diagram. First, let's take a look at a long $50 call at expiration, which we saw earlier in Chapter 3. Figure 9.1 shows the profit and loss characteristics, assuming that $3 was paid for the call:

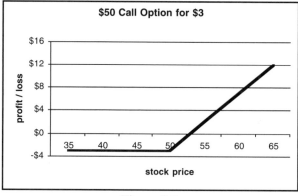

Figure 9.1

To interpret this chart, simply look at the stock prices on the horizontal axis, which range from $35 to $65. Then draw an imaginary line from the stock price directly to the profit and loss line (the dark "hockey stick" shaped line). For any stock price below $50 at expiration, we see that the profit and loss diagram lines up with a loss of $3 on the vertical axis. This is because the option loses all of its value for any stock price below $50 at expiration and expires worthless.

Consequently, the maximum that is lost to the investor is the amount paid, which is $3. However, once the stock price is above $50, the intrinsic value[18] of the option begins to offset losses and

---

[18] For call options, intrinsic value is the difference between the stock price and the strike price. If the stock is at $52, the $50 call option has $2 intrinsic value.

the position breaks even at $53, which is where the profit and loss line crosses zero on the vertical axis. Any stock price above $53 starts to produce profits (not including commissions) and we can see there is no limit to the amount of profit that could be made if the stock continues upward. You should now be able to understand the importance of profit and loss diagrams as this entire paragraph is summed up in that one simple picture.

Now let's take a look at the long stock plus long put position. Remember, we're trying to show that the long call is synthetically equal to long stock and a long put. We just saw what a long $50 call looks like in Figure 9.1, so now we need to compare that chart to one of long stock and a long put.

We know that long stock has a straight-line payoff, which we saw in Chapter 3, Figure 3.1. That means that a stockowner will make dollar-for-dollar gains and losses with the stock. However, if the investor buys a $50 put for $3, they can always use that put to sell the stock for $50. The put acts as an "insurance policy" on the stock, thus guaranteeing a minimum of $50 by expiration. Therefore, the owner of the stock cannot lose dollar-for-dollar below a price of $50. In exchange for this privilege, they must pay the $3 premium. The net result is shown in Figure 9.2:

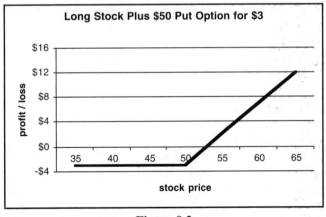

Figure 9.2

If you compare Figures 9.1 and 9.2, you will see they look exactly the same, which is why they are synthetic equivalents of each other.

We will not be getting into how to determine synthetic equivalents, although the basics presented here may provide enough insight for those with more advanced trading experience. If you wish to see the details, you can do so at our free options course at www.21stcenturyinvestor.com/page/education/tco/courses.

The only synthetic options we are concerned with are *synthetic long* and *synthetic short* positions.

Synthetic Long and Short Positions

As stated earlier, using stock, calls, and puts, a specific combination of any two will produce the synthetic equivalent of the third. We can replicate a long stock position by simply buying the call and selling the put. This is a synthetic long futures position.

We saw in Chapter 3 that a long stock or futures contract produces a straight-line profit and loss diagram as in Figure 9.3:

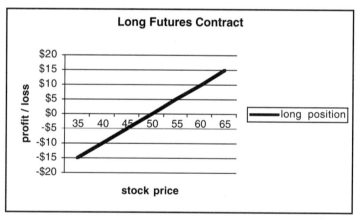

Figure 9.3

This simply shows that the stock or futures owner will gain or lose point-for-point with moves in the underlying asset. To recreate this profile synthetically, we can buy a $50 call and sell a $50 put. The net result from a profit and loss standpoint is shown in Figure 9.4:

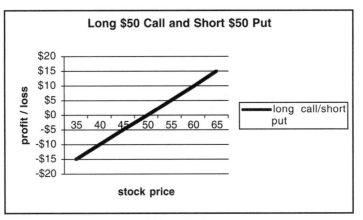

Figure 9.4

You can see that Figures 9.3 and 9.4 look exactly the same and are therefore synthetic equivalents of each other. The same logic works in reverse. We know that a short futures position looks like Figure 9.5:

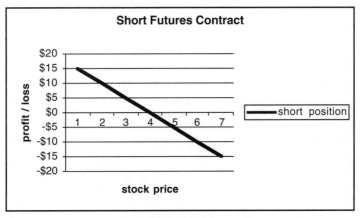

Figure 9-5

This chart just shows that a trader will gain (lose) dollar-for-dollar with decreases (increases) in the underlying asset. We can also plot the profit and loss diagram for a long $50 put and short $50 call, which is shown in Figure 9.6:

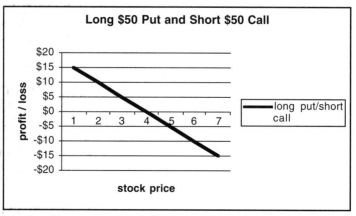

Figure 9.6

Because Figures 9.5 and 9.6 look identical, they are synthetic equivalents of each other.

Key points:

Synthetic Long Futures = Long call plus a short put

Synthetic Short Futures = Long put plus a short call

How can we use this information to hedge enter or exit futures positions? If you are long a futures contract and wish to exit a position that is locked limit for the day, you simply enter the opposite long or short position synthetically in the options market. This isn't difficult to remember if you just think about how you would normally exit the futures contract with an offsetting position. Remember that an offsetting position is a reversing trade. If you are long the futures contract, you enter an order to short that same contract — a reversing position — and you are effectively out of the contract.

Key point:
   If you are long a futures contract and wish to exit through the options market:

   Enter a synthetic short in the options market: Buy the put and sell the call.

Key point:
If you are short a futures contract and wish to exit through the options market:

Enter a synthetic long in the options market: Buy the call and sell the put.

If you cannot access the futures markets because it is locked limit trading for the day, you can quickly reverse your position by entering the opposite — or reversing — trade in the *options* market. If you were long the futures contract, you would want to short the futures synthetically in the options market to reverse your obligations. The cheapest way to accomplish this is to buy a put and sell the call with the same strike as the synthetic current level of the commodity.

How much will this cost?
Theoretically, it should be very close to zero (with the exception of commissions) if you can find strikes that are closely matched to the current level of the underlying futures contract.

For example, the underlying futures contract may be limit up at 70, but we can determine where it is trading in the minds of investors by simply looking at the options market. We may see a 72 strike for calls and puts trading at the same price. If so, we know the futures are trading synthetically at 72.

How do we know it will cost close to zero, assuming we can find the proper strikes? While this is often confusing to many people at first, it's very easy to understand. But it will help initially to think about the following analogy.

Assume you buy an item at a store, say for 70 cents. If you give the cashier 70 cents, you owe nothing and you also get no change back. That shows that the item was "trading for" exactly 70 cents. However, if you give the cashier a $1 bill you get the item with additional 30 cents cash back (credit). Paying one dollar with a credit of 30 cents shows the item was "trading for" 70 cents. In other words, you've overpaid by giving one dollar, so in order to make the trade fair the cashier owes you a credit of 30 cents.

Likewise, if you were to give the cashier 50 cents, he would not sell the item unless you paid another 20 cents (debit). If you pay 50 cents with an additional debit of 20 cents then that also shows the item is "trading for" 70 cents. Keep this example in mind as we work through the synthetic versions so we can easily see where the futures market is trading, even though we're looking at the options market.

Figure 9.7 shows a brief list of April option quotes for live cattle, which have about 25 days remaining.

Live Cattle Futures Options		
Strike	**Apr Calls**	**Apr Puts**
70	1.675	.05
71	.775	.15
72	.225	.600
73	.075	1.45
74	.025	2.40

Figure 9.7

We assumed that a short futures position was held and that we wanted to exit the position by purchasing the contract synthetically through the options market. Because we must <u>buy</u> the synthetic version, it may seem obvious that we want to pay as little as possible, such as with the 70 strikes. Remember that a $70 call gives us the right to purchase the underlying asset for 70. Many *assume* that it must be the best strike to purchase since it allows us to pay the least. We know we must enter a synthetic long futures contract, so we need to buy the call and sell the put. Using the quotes in Figure 9.7 we see we must pay $1.675 for the call and will receive .05 for the put for a net debit (payment) of $1.625. In other words, in order to buy the contract for 70, we must ante up some more money, just as we did when we tried to buy the 70-cent item in the store for 50 cents. This implies that the futures contract is trading for 70 + 1.625 = 71.625.

What if, instead, we opted for the 74 strikes on the calls and puts? Now we would pay .025 for the call but receive 2.40 for the put for a net credit of 2.375. This implies that we paid too much just as when we paid $1 for the item in the store. Since we received $2.375 change back (a credit), the value of the futures contract must be 74 - 2.375

= 71.625, which is exactly the same answer we got when we used the 70 strikes.

You can work through other examples and see that it really doesn't matter which strike we use, and it also doesn't matter whether we try to buy the item in the store for 50 cents, 70 cents, or $1. The net debits and credits that follow will balance it out to the actual value of the contract, which is shown in Figure 9.8:

Live Cattle Futures Options				
Strike	**Apr calls**	**Apr puts**	**Net credit/debit to buy call and sell puts**	**Effective purchase price**
70	1.675	.05	-1.625	71.625
71	.775	.15	-0.625	71.625
72	.225	.600	+0.375	71.625
73	.075	1.45	+1.375	71.625
74	.025	2.40	+2.375	71.625

Figure 9.8

So it appears that the futures contract should be trading for 71.625, and a quick check on the settlement price on that day (April 3, 2002) shows it was exactly 71.625. And no, these numbers were not made up. They are all actual quotes taken on the same day. The markets are just very efficient at pricing things fairly.

The quickest way to determine where the futures are trading synthetically is to find the same strike options that are trading the closest in value to each other. Using Figure 9.8 we can see that, although none are the same price, the 72 strike calls and puts are the closest in price (.225 and .600). That alone tells you the futures are trading synthetically close to 72. That's because whether we are entering a synthetic long or short position, we either buy the call and sell the put, or do the reverse; we'll owe nothing and will not receive "change" back, which means that must be the value of the commodity.

If we wish to zero-in on an exact price, we see that buying the 72 strike calls and selling the same puts results in a net credit of +0.375, which means we pay 72 - 0.375 = 71.625. Locating the pair of options that are close to the same price is the fastest way to determine where the futures are trading synthetically. In other words, if the futures were not locked limit, then 71.625 is where we would expect them to be trading.

So if this really were a short futures contract that you were trying to buy back synthetically, which strike should you use? Although it doesn't really matter mathematically, I would probably look for the contract that is most liquid (highest volume) and requires the smallest debit or credit. The reason you probably do not want a large debit or credit is because although these may seem like small amounts, remember that contract sizes can be quite large. For the cattle futures in this example, the contract size is 40,000 pounds, which means a net debit of 0.625 will cost 0.625 * 40,000 = \$25,000.

Now you may be tempted instead to take a small credit, such as 0.375. However, you will have to pay 72 (the strike) to take delivery of the long futures contract even though it was trading for 71.625 at the time you bought the contract synthetically. Once again, it doesn't really matter mathematically; you can either pay now or pay later. And don't think you can beat the market by opting to pay later. If there is significant time remaining, the cost of carry will be priced in as well.

Now you should understand what was meant by the earlier "How much will this cost?" box. If we can locate a pair of calls and puts trading for the same price, we know that strike price is where the futures are trading synthetically. At that price, you will not pay any debits and will not receive any credits. In other words, you owe nothing and you get no change back — you're paying the exact value. So ideally, most traders who use this strategy try to find the synthetic long or short version that nets a zero debit or credit.

Another reason to look for the "net zeros" is because they are more likely to get filled if the trader doesn't have to give any cash back. While it shouldn't make a difference mathematically, it does make a difference to traders who rely on large cash positions to fill orders — and not to float loans for other traders.

Additionally, with the underlying futures market locked limit up, the floor traders (called "locals") are taking in a huge order flow from others trying to do the same thing, yet the floor traders are unable to hedge off the risk like they normally do since the futures are locked.

Because of this, they will likely provide a tighter market (smaller bid-ask spreads) on the options that require no cash outlay.

Another View of Synthetic Positions

We said it didn't matter mathematically which strike you used to enter a synthetic trade. Some people are still tempted, though, to use the synthetic version that nets a credit. In the above example, they may be tempted to use the 73 strikes for a 1.375 credit thinking that if the market rises they will use the call, but if it falls they'll just keep the credit. After all, it's the rising market they are trying to hedge in this example, so if they don't need the call they will be left with a nice fat credit.

The reason this doesn't work is because you have effectively *guaranteed* the purchase at 73 by entering the synthetic long position at 73. Here's why: If the futures market rises, the call option gains value and you would certainly exercise at expiration, which means you would buy it for 73. But if the market falls, you can't just walk away with your credit. That's because you are short the put option, which gives you the *obligation to buy* at the strike price if the long put position exercises. So whether the market rises or falls, you're buying at 73! Entering into a synthetic long futures contract guarantees the purchase at the strike, which is why the strategy works in the first place. If it were not a guaranteed purchase, you couldn't say this is a way to exit the contract.

Of course, it is possible to not exercise your call, in this example, but rather just sell it in the open market to offset your losses on the short futures contract if the market rises. In this sense, the purchase of a call acts as a hedge just as we saw (in Chapter 1) how a long futures contract acts as a hedge for the spot market. The sale of the put just reduces your cost of the call to nearly nothing. Similarly, if the market falls, we could buy back the put in the open market for a loss, which will offset the gain in the short futures position. So whether you use the options to buy the futures contract or just close the options in the open market, the gain or loss is effectively locked in at the time you enter the synthetic futures position.

Please don't think that using synthetics is a way to beat the market at the futures game. It's not. However, synthetic options do provide a way to get out of a futures contract if the futures market is locked limit and the options continue to trade. So while synthetics may not provide a *cheaper* way out, at least they provide a way out. Take the time to understand the process in case you find yourself in need of using them; it will be too late to learn it at that time.

Questions

1) You are LONG a futures contract that is locked limit up for the day. However, the options on that commodity are trading. What position would you enter to exit your position through the options market?

   a) synthetic long
   b) synthetic short

2) How would you enter the position in Question #1?

   a) long call + short put
   b) long put + short call
   c) long call + long put
   d) short call + short put

3) If a futures contract is limit up or down for the day, no trades can take place on that commodity during the day.

   a) true
   b) false

4) A commodity is locked limit for the day and you are looking at option quotes to determine where the commodity is trading. How can you quickly determine that price?

   a) Find the same strike calls and puts that offer the highest credit.

   b) Find the same strike calls and puts that create the largest debit.

   c) Find the same strike calls and puts that are close to the same price.

5) In your own words, describe the meaning of a synthetic position.

Answers

1) You are LONG a futures contract that is locked limit up for the day. However, the options on that commodity are trading. What position would you enter to exit your position through the options market?

b) synthetic short

2) How would you enter the position in Question #1?

b) long put + short call

3) If a futures contract is limit up or down for the day, no trades can take place on that commodity during the day.

b) false

Trades can take place *within* the limits, just not *outside*. However, many times the liquidity will be next to nothing as the traders expect a similar move the next day.

4) A commodity is locked limit for the day and you are looking at option quotes to determine where the commodity is trading. How can you quickly determine that price?

c) Find the same strike calls and puts that are close to the same price.

5) In your own words, describe the meaning of a synthetic position.

A synthetic position is the use of a specific combination of calls and puts designed to behave, from a profit and loss standpoint, exactly like that of another position (such as a long or short futures contract).

Chapter 10
Risks and Rewards

Single-stock futures will be a new and exciting tool for hedgers and speculators alike. Despite their benefits, I often hear people criticize that adding one more investment class only adds to the confusion amongst the seemingly infinite number of choices already available. They insist there's no reason to learn about them, as they are perfectly happy with their stocks, bonds, and options.

Before you accept that line of thought, we're going to show you how market participants respond to any financial investment. It does not matter if it is new, such as single-stock futures, or an existing one, such as stocks and bonds. The method of pricing all assets depends on risk and return. To demonstrate how this is done, we're going to look at some gambling games just to make it fun. As we will find out, even games of chance are priced according to risk.

How Much Would You Pay?

Assume two games are offered, and in order to play you must bid on a ticket for that game. Only the top 100 bids will be accepted. If you win one of the top 100 spots, you are allowed to play that game. The following two games are offered:

Game 1: A coin is flipped. If the coin lands heads, each player wins $10. If it lands tails, each player loses the price he paid for the ticket.

Game 2: A six-sided die is rolled and, if it lands on the number 6, each player wins $10, otherwise each player loses the price he paid for the ticket.

Also assume there are hundreds of thousands of people willing to play, but only 100 people can play at a time and they are free to compete on price. Only the 100 highest bidders are allowed to play the game at any one time.

What can we expect to see happen with the prices of these two games? Before reading on, take a close look at the two games above and think about them for a moment. Which would you prefer to play? How will this preference affect its price? Once you've thought about it, continue reading and see if you have the right answers.

First of all, we see that both have the same $10 payoff. However, each is subject to a different set of risks. Even if you do not have an understanding of probabilities, you should be able to deduce that you would win far more often playing the first game. On average, you would win the first game every other time and win the second game every sixth time. In other words, the second carries more uncertainty — it is riskier. Because the frequency of wins is higher in the first, everybody prefers to play that game over the second one for any given cost.

While the fair price of this game can be found mathematically, we're going to assume that the gamblers have no such knowledge and must learn by trial and error.

Let's say that the first several rounds of the game are played with each gambler paying $1 for the ticket. On average, the gamblers will pay $1 every time but will win $10 every other time. In other words, the gamblers will pay $2 to win $10, on average. This makes for a net gain of $8 every two games or $4 per game.

We can show this result mathematically by looking at what are called expected values, which are nothing more than the sum of the gains and losses multiplied by their probabilities. Using expected values, we can show that half the time the gamblers will lose their dollar and half the time they will make $9 (pay $1 to play and receive $10):

$$- \$1 \ (1/2) = -\$.50$$
$$+\$9 \ (1/2) = +\$4.50$$
$$\text{Net} = +\$4 \text{ per game}$$

Regardless of how you look at it, the gamblers can expect an average gain of $4 per game. Because they expect net profits, they continue to play. The other gamblers not playing this game will see the profits mounting and become eager to play, but they cannot because all 100 seats are filled. In order to play, they must bid higher than the going rate of $1. If the game is now bid to $2.00, the expected return to the gamblers becomes:

$$- \$2 \ (1/2) = -\$1$$
$$+\$8 \ (1/2) = +\$4$$
$$\text{Net} = +\$3 \text{ per game}$$

The additional dollar bid is countered by an additional dollar less of expected profit. The expected gain falls from $4 to $3. Still, the spectator gamblers see the profits continuing, although not as fast, so they continue to bid up the price to play. Eventually, the price will be bid to $5 to the point where gamblers can expect to break even, on average:

$$- \$5 \ (1/2) = -\$2.5$$
$$+\$5 \ (1/2) = +\$2.5$$
$$\text{Net} = \$0 \text{ per game}$$

At a bid of $5 per game, the gamblers are expected to neither win nor lose in the long run. If they bid $5 to play, they will lose $5 half the time and gain $5 half of the time. If the bids rise above this amount, even to just $5.01, the house would start to earn money per game (the gamblers would lose), on average, and the gamblers would learn to reduce their bets. So we find that in the long run the first game will be bid to a value of $5 and stay in equilibrium at that level. There is no incentive for gamblers to bid higher and no room to bid lower. If one gambler bids less than $5, another gambler will be willing to bid $5 to take his place.

What happens to the price of the second game? At some point through all of this bidding in the first game, some gamblers will try the second game but will never bid more than the price of the first game. Remember, the first game is preferred for any given price because of the reduced risk. Therefore, the second game will never have a value greater than the first. However, this does not mean it will have no value. Gamblers will give it a try at some point.

Let's assume gamblers are able to participate by only paying one dollar. The gamblers who bid $1 will lose, on average, every five out of six games. Every sixth game, on average, they will pay their $1 fee but win $10 for a net gain of $9.

$$- \$1 \ (5/6) = -\$0.83$$
$$\underline{+ \ \$9 \ (1/6) = +\$1.50}$$
$$\text{Net} = +\$0.67 \text{ per game}$$

This net expected gain is small but still positive, so gamblers will continue to bid up its price. From what we learned in the first game, we know that if there is a net expected gain, the gamblers will continue to bid higher. How much room is left for them to bid? Exactly the amount of the net expected gain. Because an expected gain of 0.67 remains after bidding $1, they will eventually bid this game to a price of $1.67. At that price, there will be no incentive to bid it higher and no room to bid it lower:

$$- \ \$1.67 \ (5/6) = -\$1.3916$$
$$\underline{+ \ \$8.33 \ (1/6) = +\$1.3883}$$
$$\text{Net} = \$0.0033 \text{ per game, which is approximately zero.}[19]$$

When the price is in equilibrium, no gambler will bid it higher; and if they bid lower, another gambler will quickly take their place by bidding higher. The end result is that the first game will be bid to a value of $5 and the second to a value of $1.67. We could also rationalize another way. The second game would take three times as long to win, on average, than the first. In the first game, gamblers could expect to win every two turns while those playing the second game could expect to win every six turns, which is exactly one-third as often. Because both games pay out $10, the value of the second game must be one-third that of the first or $5/3 = $1.67.

Efficient Market Theory

What we just demonstrated is a variation of a well-known financial theory called the Efficient Market Theory (EMT). While there are three different forms of EMT, the one we demonstrated is known

---

[19] The reason it is not exactly zero is due to rounding. If we could assume that gamblers could split cents and pay amounts such as $1.6666667, we could then get the expected payout to exactly balance to zero.

as the semi-strong form and states that all publicly available information is priced into each and every asset just as was done with our gambling games. We can demonstrate EMT with a simpler version too by asking a simple question, "Is it better to own a Porsche Boxster or a Ford Taurus?" Although I'm sure you have an immediate answer, the correct answer may surprise you.

Many people are tempted to answer that the Porsche is clearly the better choice.

To find out if that's true, let's start by assuming that both the Ford Taurus and Porsche Boxster are both priced the same. With both cars priced the same, few would disagree that you are better off with the Porsche. If so, people will buy the Porsche over the Taurus. This will put buying pressure on the Porsche and raise its price relative to the Taurus. Say the Porsche is now bid up to a price $3,000 above the Taurus. Most would agree that it is still a better deal and continue to buy it. This action will continue until the markets are not so sure that an additional $1 is worth jumping from the Taurus to the Boxster. If it were worth it, they would do it.

While it may go against your intuition, as long as there is no net bidding up or down of prices between the two cars, you are equally well off with either one. While the Porsche may be faster and have higher quality and resale value (not to mention it just looks cooler), it also comes with higher repair bills, insurance rates and theft occurrences. The car market will reflect all pros and cons in the prices of the two cars. Similarly, the financial markets will price all assets to reflect their risks. Quality assets are bid up and riskier assets are sold off.

This is why a government T-bill yielding 5% is equal to a more risky bond priced to yield 10%. The government bond is higher quality but also has a lower yield. The markets realize that, all else constant, you are better off with the T-bill; so you will continue to bid that price up until there is no net difference between the two bonds. If there were an advantage, the markets would continue taking action and reflect it in the price.

The important point to draw from this is that all markets, whether stocks, bonds, options, futures, real estate, coins, art — even casinos

— will be priced according to risk. Granted, the financial markets are not as easy to price as the two gambling games we presented that offer a precise payout with exact probabilities. Nonetheless, the principle is the same. Investors will bid the price up if they feel there is more reward (or less risk) and bid the price down if there is less reward (or more risk), as was done with these two gambling games.

Single-stock futures are just one of many investment markets and will be priced according to risk. Do not be fooled by people who say they are too risky or that they are not worth learning. Just as with our gambling games, even though the second game was riskier didn't mean that gamblers would not play it. They'll play for the right price. Whatever that price may be is up to the market to decide. The same holds true for single-stock futures. They have a unique set of risks and rewards that is unavailable with any other asset. Consequently, they will carry a price to reflect those risks and rewards.

Single-stock futures are simply another investment "game" out of many from which you can choose. If you choose to not allow single-stock futures into your investment portfolio, or to not entertain the idea of learning about them, you are essentially blocking out the advantages they may offer in a particular situation. What's worse is that you will probably substitute them with a less efficient product to accomplish the same task. If you avoid learning about them you will exclude yourself from being able to use these new and innovative tools, designed to efficiently help you control risk.

As the famous psychologist, Abraham Maslow, once said, " To the man who only has a hammer in the toolkit, every problem looks like a nail." Without single-stock futures in your toolkit, the investor who only uses stocks, bonds, or options will see those particular assets as the solution to every financial problem. If that were the case, then the other assets in the market would never have come into existence. Single-stock futures are the answer to a long-term problem of hedging risk. They allow us to quickly spread that risk off to speculators who are willing to accept it. They allow the investor or speculator to custom tailor risk and reward profiles using methods that are much less efficient without them. They are not a pointless product designed by brokers to sell, nor were they created under political pressures of the wealthy as a means to legally gamble for the fun of it.

The markets created them out of necessity. Single-stock futures can be used to hedge risk conservatively or to speculate wildly, among its uses within every shade of gray in between. The choice of how to use them is up to you — assuming you decide to use them. If you choose not to, you will leave behind an invaluable tool that allows you to be more proficient at maneuvering through the volatile conditions and uncertainties that exist in today's complex markets. I'm convinced that using single stock futures will be essential for more successful investing.

I hope you are convinced, too.

INDEX

Entries followed by *f* and *n* refer to figures and notes respectively.